Keeping STUDENTS from DROPPING OUT of post-secondary occupational education REVISED

Practical Guidelines & Tested Proposals

by Richard N. Diggs

This Guide will be helpful to the conscientious personnel of our proprietary schools in the neverending fight to control attrition. And to the concerned occupational educator in the public system, whose challenge is greater yet!

Copyright 1988, by Richard N. Diggs
All rights reserved, including the right of reproduction in whole or in part without written permission of the publisher.

For information, call or write:
Progressive Publications
P.O. Box 4016
Homosassa Springs, FL 32647
(904) 382-1452

Printed in the United States of America
ISBN 0-937157-04-X

Library of Congress Catalog Card Number 88-92441

Original edition copyright 1979

Contents

1. Why It Is Increasingly Important To Establish Your Own Plan To Prevent Attrition 1
2. Let's Understand Why Students Drop Out! 7
3. Care Enough To Give The Very Best 11
4. Gathering A Staff That Cares 14
5. Keeping Staff Morale High 22
6. Creating A Home Away From Home 29
7. Know Your Attrition Rates 34
8. Recruiting With Dropouts In Mind 36
9. Being Aware Of Potential Dropouts 46
10. Preventing Cancellations And No Shows 52
11. Comprehensive Orientation — A Must! 58
12. Greeting, Impressing, And Communicating With Your New Students 65
13. Your Attendance Policy 70
14. Sound Course Objectives 76
15. Dynamic Instruction — The Backbone Of Education 78

16. Student—Management Communications 97
17. The Importance Of The Student Counselor 102
18. Counseling Relevant To
    Establishing Career Objectives 105
19. The Science of Placement ... Perhaps The
    Most Misunderstood And Neglected Function On
    U.S. Campuses, Yet The Single-Most Important
    Factor In Controlling Attrition 114
20. Counseling Relevant To Problem Solving 123
21. Student Morale—Creating It, Keeping It! 130
22. Should Students Interrupt —
    Leave The Door Open 139
23. Assisting The Slow Learner And Those In Need
    Of Remedial Assistance 142
24. The Inner City Student 145
25. Tuition—Its Effect On Attrition 149
26. Support Vocational Education — And
    The Job Done By Proprietary Schools 151
27. When Dropping A Student Is Advisable 155
    Conclusion 159

Acknowledgement

The successful pursuit of any goal is never a singular endeavor. Many have joined in this particular effort: The hundreds of educators, both from the public and private sector, who unselfishly shared their ideas, suggestions, and experiences. Alice Diamond, Al Pribish, Doug Davies, Bill Goddard, and Lance Coalson, who provided very special guidance and counsel. Many good friends who simply offered encouragement. And wife Shirley, who stands behind me, quietly providing direction.

This book is from all of us.

Preface

Jackie had passed the midway point in his occupational course. He was succeeding as never before. For an inner-city black who had dropped out of high school, Jackie had already accomplished more than many of his peers ever would. But he was solemn when contemplating a future that was now realistically obtainable. Beyond the paycheck, beyond being a member of society, was the haunting fact that he would have to subscribe to regimentation and discipline and a lengthy uphill climb, from an entry-level wage to perhaps an average living. "Hell, I did better working the streets!" Jackie exclaimed, and added as he walked away: "I just don't know if it's worth it to stick around!"

Our students are filled with doubts and fears and overtaken by futility and premature decisions. In our nation's schools, thousands of similar stories are inscribed daily. Among these tales of giving up no two are alike. Yet if viewed in the mass as the social disorder they surely constitute, these dropouts would long ago have been rightly labeled as "reaching epidemic proportions."

And how strange it is that, for the most part, the educators (both public and private) of our country will work intensely to get students in the front door, while at least 30 to 50 percent of their recruits are disappearing through the back door—seldom with as much as a word of good-bye!

The effect of this massive exodus from training and from education is a tragic loss of fulfillment. Tragic for the students, their families, and society. It is as well an awesome loss of revenue to these students, our schools, and our government both in squandered federal aid for education and in the loss of many who could have expanded the nation's work force and become contributors rather than recipients.

This book is dedicated to reducing attrition. Although the ideas herein have mostly been drawn from the experiences of post-secondary education, certainly there is reason to believe that much of what is presented is applicable to education at all levels.

As a former member of an accrediting commission, I have often been asked: "What should our attrition rate be?" As though an acceptable figure could be targetted. But my reply has always been the same. "Your rate of attrition should be the figure you arrive at, AFTER you have implemented and exhausted every means known to man to reduce it."

No two schools are the same. Whether or not you have considered your school different, you may believe you are indeed unique. The problems faced by your staff and your students are similarly "one of a kind" and as such, you must formulate your own plan. On the following pages you will find many suggestions which might fit into your blueprint. Try them. Keep trying. Devise your own. In any case don't be guilty of the same thing you are attempting to prevent,—"giving up."

Unfortunately it's an unrelenting problem, that attitudinally must be approached as a weight-watcher observes food: To take it off and keep it off requires constant vigilance. Fortunately there are ample rewards for both.

Chapter 1

Why It Is Becoming Increasingly Important To Establish Your Own Plan To Prevent Attrition

Today we often hear stories of apathy that send chills reverberating through our bodies. Someone dies or is injured severely while others watch, not choosing to get involved. They excused themselves as if man has no responsibility to man. When reading about something like this most of us find it hard to understand. We immediately pass judgement, condemning these cold, heartless observers, knowing full well we would not have allowed the tragedy to occur.

One day, I was driving to work after reading of a young girl being attacked in broad daylight by a defiant gang. I thought in depth about my actions. If I were there, would I really have done any different than those who watched? I frankly didn't know. The more I thought about it the more I thought a person would actually have to live through such an experience to know his own reactions.

I pulled into my parking space, then walked slowly into my school, still kicking thoughts around as to my own concern for others. It wasn't long before I began to think about the failures I observed each day; students who were no longer with us as the result of their environment, their upbringing, their prior education, the bigotry of society, their appearance, their physical or mental handicaps. What was my feeling for them? Did I shed any tears when they left? No I hadn't. Furthermore I had to admit that in most cases I was glad they left. THEY WERE THE PROBLEMS I COULD WELL DO WITHOUT.

I felt a little ashamed. How many kids had I observed crying for help, even screaming for help whom I had allowed to walk out my door knowing full well they were destined for mediocrity or less. Who was I kidding? I interpreted those cries for assistance yet I pretended not to hear.

An old saying came readily to mind: "To clean up the world, start with sweeping your own doorstep." I promised myself to do better. The thought of being a hypocrite annoyed me. As long as I can remember I've heard people say, "Why doesn't somebody do something about that!" And every time I heard this, I would smile and say to myself, "How come you don't do something yourself, wiseguy?" Well now it was my turn to ask myself, "Why don't I do something?" From then on I vowed our school would assist all students in trouble. THEIR PROBLEMS WOULD BE OUR PROBLEMS. No one will leave us before we've at least had a crack at seeking solutions. A pleasant thought came to mind. "Their success is our success."

Over the years we initiated many policies which we felt would keep students. We learned a great deal. In particular one very pleasant fact: "When you help a student you help your school."

This might not make a bad motto for your staff to keep in mind. The future of any private school may well depend on the faithful allegiance of your former students. Their recommendations could spell the difference between solvency and premature retirement. Within a short time, apathy at any school could become a luxury none of us can afford!

I believe it is now becoming increasingly more important for any school to formulate a plan to prevent attrition. Economics will demand it. My reasons are as follows:

1. GOVERNMENT REQUIREMENTS

As long as government funds are used to assist those who are attending our schools, there will be politicians and bureaucrats who will be screaming for more rigid regulations.

Among the "hot" topics that always seems to be on the table are rates of retention and default rates. At any future time, either could be the reason your school is denied further eligibility to participate in Federal programs.

In some cases there is certainly strength to their argument. A recent U.S. General Accounting Office report submitted to the Chairman of the House Subcommittee on Postsecondary Education revealed that 35% of all vocational student borrowers defaulted on their Federal loans.

Poor default rates, alone, are difficult to defend. They are simply black and white figures on paper. But they are often closely related to retention. One problem causes the other.

And what the screamers seldom understand is that there is no way one retention rate or a pattern of rates can be established that is equitable for all schools. No two schools are alike. Clientele, geography, subject matter, course length, student ages, financial structure, weather, etc., etc., give credence to the validity of the argument that specific mandated rates for retention are not feasible or reasonable.

Unfortunately, such logic can only be understood by those who have lived in the vocational school environment or gained first-hand knowledge through visitations and study.

Chances are that those who might lobby for sweeping regulations will have no such insight. But this is certainly no indication that they couldn't succeed.

Your best defense is not in exercising your vocal chords, but in the employment of every means at your disposal to reduce your attrition. Solve your drop-out problem and chances are you'll lower your default rate at the same time.

2. COMPETITION

Since the accrediting standards were relaxed in the mid-1980's to allow for widespread establishment of auxiliary campuses, the total number of private occupational schools has multiplied at an astounding rate.

So we have many more schools operating in a market that will remain relatively the same in total numbers through the year 2000 at which time it will begin a slow but steady decline.

The competition will be intense. Even after your students arrive on your campus, you can be sure that there will be opportunists still calling them to induce them to go elsewhere.

3. OUR YOUTH NEED TO GAIN SKILLS

As technology continues to act as a catalyst for industry, fewer jobs are available to the unskilled. This particularly affects the youth in our major cities who continue to drop out of our "nothing in it for me" high schools at rates up to 50%. Looking for any kind of job is now further complicated by both unions and government regulations, and the meager wages available. Even if a job is to be found, it hardly can compare with the near riskless and profitable occupation of crime.

Our courts are a joke. So much so that "getting away with murder" is no longer just an expression. A New York State Select Committee on crime investigation revealed these incomprehensible facts: Today about one in three felonies is reported. One in three reported crimes leads to an arrest. Slightly more than half of all arrests lead to indictments. One in three indictments results in conviction. And one in six convictions ends in incarceration. This means the average juvenile who commits a major felony has only one chance in a hundred of serving time. Even if he or she is convicted, and even if the crime is homicide, the average sentence is under two years. The investigation also showed that juveniles arrested for homicide were repeatedly released to the streets.

Crime does pay. Considering this, combined with the unavailability of jobs, it's hardly any wonder why our teenage jobless rate is now higher than at anytime since the 1930's.

The path to "go straight" is also barred by the apparent results of disinterest and bigotry in public education. For example, even the ambitious Job Corps program of "The Great Society" failed to show any measurable results, despite enormous cost.

The ingenuity and genuine concern of the proprietary occupational school can be a wedge to help reverse this tragic pattern. The public schools—with their course inflexibility, fixed budgets, tenure problems, inability to discipline, red-tape procedures and general apathy—cannot begin to find the solutions.

In this vein, the right to enroll high school dropouts as eligible recipients of federal assistance must continue to be a major priority of the private occupational school industry. And once these students are enrolled, every effort must be made to see that they stay through graduation. Society cannot tolerate more youth without skills, walking the streets.

The Vocational Foundation Inc., in New York, a 40-year old agency dedicated to finding jobs for troubled young people, now says the problem is beyond their reach. "We have a national state of emergency."

These aimless youth are gathering and festering joblessly in all our major cities. As time passes, they become more deeply estranged from the laws and the institutions of our society. But they are Americans and to ignore them is to advocate violence, sickness and hopelessness.

The concerned management of proprietary occupational schools can provide hope for many. It is a challenge and an opportunity that if accepted carries an obligation to save individual lives and perhaps cities.

Survival is now the name of the game. Either we provide the means to survive or it will be taken from us.

4. INFLATION

The private school offering postsecondary education becomes subjected to stiffer competition as the tuition gap between public and private schools gets wider and wider. Inflation makes it difficult for any small business to stay afloat. Inflation combined with the fact we must compete with public education is like trying to take a canoe upstream without oars. Recent history has shown that tuition rates at public postsecondary schools have not increased at the same rate as the cost of living. Most of the increases have been passed along to the taxpayer. Tuition rates at many private postsecondary schools are now five times greater than their public competition.

It doesn't take a genius to realize that as this gap continues to widen, private schools must not only do a superior job of recruiting and training but they must do everything possible to keep every student in school.

5. PUBLIC RELATIONS

It seems as though every time our Industry is mentioned in the press, the negative messages delivered to the public far exceed the positive.

If collectively, we all strive to keep our students in school, not only will we start to gain the ear of those who now consider us suspect, but we will assure ourselves participation in future government assistance programs.

Chapter 2

Let's Understand Why Students Drop Out!

During the course of gathering resource material for this book, letters of opinion were generously sent from just about every state in the country. Not surprisingly, many started out with an enumeration of the causes of attrition. Many more simply stated they were to numerous to mention. None said that in reality there are just a couple reasons why students drop out, yet that is the opinion of this writer.

You can make a list based on what your dropouts have disclosed and it will run in length about as long as a ledger of those who cheated on their income tax last year, but just how valid is it? You're right! It's about as believable as the explanation of a man who's just been caught cheating on his wife. The valid accumulation of data is further mired in doubt by the fact that many students themselves don't actually know why they are dropping out. They often will give the response, "Oh, it's many things," and they'll go on to blame this, that and the other thing. When you come right down to it though, an accurate assessment of all their excuses might well be boiled down to this: THE STUDENTS DROPPED OUT BECAUSE THEY DIDN'T VIEW THEIR EDUCATIONAL EXPERIENCE AS THE MAJOR PRIORITY IN THEIR LIVES.

Let's take this thought and expand on it more specifically. One of the major causes for attrition which appears on just about every school's list is "Financial." You can participate in every federal plan available and you'll still get this excuse; "I just can't afford it!"

Well you know as well as anyone that if you're an accredited school with financial aid personnel of even mediocre ability, no student is completely without funds, or access to them. What then is his or her money being spent on if not tuition? The answer is obvious. He or she is spending money on something he or she considers more important.

Yes, very often they have monthly financial obligations that exceed their income but if you've examined an applicant's ability to pay prior to enrollment, then much of the indebtedness occurred after starting school and if so the choice the student had was paying for either this or that. Very often a new car vs. tuition, better housing vs. tuition, an active social life vs. tuition, etc. What are we saying? Just this: The student was not convinced that the educational experience was more important than any alternative he or she had for spending what was available to spend.

Basic psychology tells us that "man never does anything intentionally he does not want to do."

When first hearing this statement many will say "nonsense" and start citing examples like: taking out the garbage, going to their kid's violin recital, or attending a ballet on the same night the heavyweight championship fight is on TV. But think a minute, what were the alternatives? Garbage in the house, bugs, the odor, the wrath of your spouse, the love and respect of your child, peace in the family, a concession you'll benefit from later.

Even a man faced with a long prison term confronts it willingly when faced with the alternative of suicide or getting killed trying to escape.

Presuming, therefore, we are correct with this assumption, it follows that: *"The only way under high heaven to get anyone to do anything is by making that person want to do it!"*

Applying this to the business of keeping students in school we conclude: Students will remain on campus if, when faced with an alternative, they choose to stay because they want to stay.

Make sense? We certainly hope so, for the remainder of this book deals with the myriad of things you can do to make your school and your training more desirable. An experience so enjoyable, in fact, that it overshadows the benefits of a new car, fancy apartment, a stereo system or any other alternative that would necessitate spending dollars otherwise ear-marked for tuition.

To establish a pattern for charting your attrition in the future you might consider two major categories: AVOIDABLE and UNAVOIDABLE. By doing so you can better measure your effectiveness with all those who could realistically be considered AVOIDABLE, and this should certainly be your largest category.

Only those who drop without having a clear-cut alternative should be labeled UNAVOIDABLE. This would include those mentally and physically disabled, deportation, incarceration or any other factor in which the student did not have the opportunity to make an intentional choice.

By no means, however, should we ignore this category by dismissing them as simply unavoidable. The title only serves to categorize your attrition AFTER the fact. Each case in this category should be analyzed as to whether attrition could have been prevented by foresight and personal concern.

Reports provided annually by the Carnegie Forum on Education and the Economy in Washington, D.C. indicate that 60% of all those starting higher education each year fail to achieve their educational objectives. "Most of these dropouts leave without formal recognition for their efforts, and many have a sense of disappointment and even resentment."

Certainly much of this resentment results from the student's sudden awareness that he or she is not educationally prepared to handle the challenge of postsecondary education. This is particularly evident in those who come from large inner-city public schools.

The challenge to compensate for their educational deficiency is too great for most - and having no one who cares specifically about them, encouraging, prodding, motivating, they give up.

Unfortunately, most who label themselves teachers say "good riddance" as the struggling student is a nuisance, a time consumer, a class disrupter, a pain in the neck!

What a country this would be if we could rid ourselves of these hypocrites; if we could somehow demand that ATTITUDE be the foremost prerequisite for those who stand before a class.

The advantage to the proprietary school in advancing such policy is evident. Realizing the causes for attrition, it can adapt. Realizing the necessity for income to exist, it must adapt.

Having a faculty and staff comprised of those WHO CARE, whether by reason of free enterprise or not, is more essential now than at any time in the history of this country. We can no longer tolerate growing numbers to be educated to take from society, rather than to contribute to it.

An easily understood parallel to school attrition is the divorce rate. Why does one partner leave? Because he or she is not happy and would prefer to be somewhere else. The student who walks out does so for the the identical reason.

The challenge we have as educators, therefore, is really quite simple: WE MUST MAKE STUDENTS WANT TO STAY IN SCHOOL!

Chapter 3

Care Enough
To Give
The Very Best

The Hallmark card people have done well with this saying, and I can think of no better phrase to adopt as the staff philosophy which will best reduce attrition.

Throughout my lifetime I have found no synonym that comes closer to describing love than the word giving.

I have also noted that the happiest people I have ever come across have also been the most generous. And being happy people they seem to have more friends, more joys, more breaks, more good fortune. We envy them, but seldom acknowledge or realize why. We speak of them as lucky, and wonder why we don't receive blessings and benefits in like manner. We often resent the gifts bestowed on others, and we blame anyone or anything for the meagerness of what comes our way. We complain and fashion a perpetual mood of self-pity. We blind ourselves to the fact "getting follows giving."

Without a doubt, the most significant day of my life occurred after spending six fruitless years of my youth searching for green grass. I was 24 and destitute, having wandered from coast to coast looking for opportunity to be cast upon me as if by the dictate of some unseen power. I slept in barns, used cars and begged money for food. I verbally chastised those who ignored my pleas, just as I found fault with all who turned their backs on me when I requested employment "cause I need the money."

Looking back, it is difficult to comprehend how I could have been so stupid for so long. I blamed my parents, and friends of my parents. I blamed all my other relatives. I blamed my former employers and society and God Almighty. Oh how I blamed God Almighty. How He directed that I should have been born both poor and ugly and have no friends in the world was unjust, unreasonable, unexplainable. But then on this one beautiful day, He explained.

I was sitting on the back steps of an abandoned building in the slums of Covington, Kentucky. As was my custom, I was neck deep in self-sympathy, lamenting life and loneliness with the ever-present thought, "Nobody loves me!" And the answer came. That single thought that changed my life: "If nobody loves you, perhaps it's because you are not loveable!"

For the first time in my 24 years, I started to look within for solutions. It dawned on me that never, in all the years I asked people to give me a break, did I ever ask myself "Why should they?"

Within hours, I had formed the new philosophy on life I have lived with since. Whatever is to be, I must make happen. I will no longer be dependent on others to chart the course of my life. I alone will determine my own destiny. I will be the best at whatever I choose to do. I will be wanted for what I have become. I will sow seeds, then reap the harvest. I will give, then I will get.

This thinking fits well into our business of retaining students. If you care enough to give the very best, your school's popularity will not only attract students, it will keep them there. So much so your peers will then consider you "lucky."

Keith Fenton, President of the American Institute of Business, expresses his school's philosophy in one statement to his staff: "What is best for the student is best for the institution. Give $2.00 of education for each $1.00 of tuition."

A similar philosophy is advocated by John Cowan, president of the Bryman School in Salt Lake City: "If the institution does not continue to motivate the student feels let down, discouraged, and heads out the back door. Educational institutions must be professional in what they teach, how they teach, and the manner in which they carry on their relationship with each student. The administration of any educational institution must show a sincere interest in the students' well-being, as well as their academic progress."

Each member of your staff who comes in contact with students carries the entire reputation of your school with him or her. Disagreements with but one individual can result in a prompt withdrawal, but even worse, a dissatisfied customer is seldom silent when contemplating his experience.

"With every failure comes an excuse!" Ever notice that! It's a fact of human behavior. The student who leaves under adverse conditions will most often absolve himself of blame. "The school ain't worth a damn!" The individual staff member may even be depicted as the villain, but it makes no difference. The image of the entire school suffers.

Make sure your school philosophy is in print and every member of your staff, from the office girl to the janitor, is well aware of the meaning and logic behind it!

Chapter 4

Gathering A Staff That Cares

School philosophies are certainly worth having. They make such fine plaques. Similarly, their value in public relations and in catalog advertising is noteworthy. However, unless backed by the actions of all employees, the philosophy of the school can result in disillusioning student opinion.

All of us find happiness in anticipation. All of us find dejection when that which is anticipated does not become reality.

An unsupported philosophy can, accordingly, cause negative reaction and an exodus of students who will thereafter speak of you as "all traction, no action," as a dealer in unfulfilled promises. To gain a reputation for "telling it like it is" can serve you well. Hypocrisy only serves to hasten retirement.

When advocating a philosophy in print, therefore, let it be a fact. Create a staff which collectively gives. One which truly thinks first of student success. This, of course, is simple to say but a task that by any measure is a formidable challenge.

The following outline of hiring practices probably is a vast departure from the procedure you've used in the past, — but it is one you should consider in light of your conscientious involvement, and bearing in mind how the people working for you will determine your success or failure, your retention or your attrition. No aspect of your business is more important than staff recruitment.

On this subject, Joe Belliotti, owner of the Sawyer School in Centerline, Michigan, offers this sound observation: "Staff attitudes are in direct relation to student attitudes. For every action there is a reaction. Positive actions cause positive reactions, but just as easily, negative actions bring about negative reactions."

This should particularly be kept in mind when hiring an instructor. At an ACT seminar on attrition I attended some time ago, I picked up a flyer that should be hung on the office wall of every school administrator in this country. It read as follows:

> YOUR GREATEST CONTRIBUTION TO MANKIND
> IS TO BE SURE THERE IS A TEACHER IN EVERY CLASSROOM
> WHO CARES THAT EVERY STUDENT
> EVERY DAY LEARNS AND GROWS AND FEELS
> LIKE A REAL HUMAN BEING

M.E. Riley, president of A.T.E.S. Technical School in Youngstown, Ohio, shares this reflection: "Almost everyone who looks back to when he was in school remembers the teacher who was perhaps strict in discipline, but who cared, made you work a little harder but showed appreciation for what you did, I sure want to be remembered as such a teacher!"

As administrators we might all do well to think back - examining the attributes of those we idolized, of those who taught us well - prior to hiring our next instructor.

Many employers are like the bride or groom who take the wedding vows with the idea they will start changing their partner after the ceremony. Ridiculous. Take the following precautions. And get the right person to begin with. All the silk purses I've ever seen have been made out of silk.

1. DETERMINE WHAT YOU NEED.
A. Make a list of all the duties the ideal employee could hopefully handle.

B. Determine what educational background should be required.

C. Determine what age group is most desirable to fit in with co-workers.

D. Determine what job experience is desired.

E. Determine what wage range you can offer and where a good employee can advance to, should he or she prove to be exemplary.

Caution:It is possible to hire people who are overqualified as well as those who are underqualified. In either case you will probably be filling out forms for the local unemployment office before long.

2. RECRUIT IN QUANTITY

Only when you have a fairly large number of candidates for a job can you exercise any degree of selectivity. When you have only one or two people to choose from, the common tendency is to compromise the requirements of the job and "make do" with what you have. In so doing, however, you short-change not only yourself but the applicant. Follow these rules:

A. Pre-determine how many applicants you intend to interview. Never less than three; twenty if you can.

B. Plan ahead, if possible. To wait until an opening occurs invites a frenzied recruiting that is not conducive to getting the best! Even if the opening occurs suddenly, however, don't hasten your decision.

C. Spend some time making a list of all sources from which good applicants can be drawn.

   1. Referrals by associates.
   2. Upgrading present staff.
   3. Newspapers.
   4. Employment agencies.

5. Trade journals.
6. College placement bureaus.
7. Civic and business organizations.

3. SCREEN FOR QUALITY

The whole recruiting and selection process is aimed at one goal; to secure a new person who CAN do the job and WILL do the job. Effective interviews, however, cannot be accomplished without following steps which are aimed at progressively eliminating the less qualified until only one or two outstanding qualified people remain.

You might consider the following steps:

A. Prepare a Preliminary Interview check list. Your time is valuable, consequently, you can't spend it interviewing every caller in depth. Prepare your list by noting basic "musts" of the job. As you progress through your list, make notes on each basic question, rating responses favorable, questionable, or unfavorable. As you end your questioning you should be able to make a quick decision as to whether the caller should be invited to come in for a second interview. If so, ask him or her to bring references, a resume and any other items that he or she believes could attest to his or her ability, character, or personality. If not, handle the caller with tact.

B. Have the applicant fill out your application. Check this and all other items he or she has brought. Note the applicant's:

   1. Thoroughness (all items answered).
   2. Neatness, spelling.
   3. Gaps in employment history.
   4. Sufficient personal and business references provided with addresses and phone numbers.
   5. Education.
   6. Extra-curricular involvement.
   7. Indications of personal philosophy; religion, morals, unionism, bigotry, attitude, race relations, business, etc.

C. Hold an "In Depth" interview. The purpose of this interview is to thoroughly probe and explore a candidate's capacity to perform the job in terms of background, training, experience, knowledge, judgement, and willingness to perform it in terms of his interests, attitudes, and beliefs. In addition, the "In Depth" interview provides an opportunity to thoroughly explore the job with the candidate and to explain in detail the scope of the opportunity, the nature of the work, the training provided, company policies, salary range, etc. The "In Depth" interview is the most important single step you will make in the screening process.

Interviewing, like selling, is both an art and a skill. In each, a high degree of proficiency can be obtained by following sound principles and basic techniques developed over many years. The following suggestions, while primarily applicable to the "In Depth" interview, can be followed equally in the preliminary phone interview.

1. PREPARE YOURSELF
   Study the application and information presented by the candidate.

2. PROVIDE FOR PRIVACY
   Select a location that will assure privacy without interruption. Inform your staff to hold all phone calls.

3. PUT THE CANDIDATE AT EASE
   Some small talk, a smile and humor will help. Explain that all candidates will be asked the same questions you are about to ask.

4. LET THE CANDIDATE DO MOST OF THE TALKING
   A major fault of most interviewers is that they tend to dominate the conversation. Don't. Keep in mind that the more the candidate talks the more he will reveal hidden but significant aspects of his personality and background. Your talking should be confined primarily to significant questions, clarifying statements, and keeping the interview from going too far afield.

5. DON'T PUSH, BUT DON'T LET IT DRAG
   If at any time during the interview you have concluded this person is not what you want then wind up as quickly as possible. Be sure to thank him for his interest and explain you feel the job does not suit his qualifications.

6. ASK QUESTIONS NATURALLY
   All questions, particularly those of a personal nature, should be asked in a normal conversational manner with an attitude which assumes you fully expect to get the information you're seeking. You should work from a list of predesigned questions, but by no means should you read from the list. In this day and age when you might be cited for employment practices it is advisable to simply ask all-inclusive questions that will divulge the answers you want without having asked the question. For example; "Tell me about yourself!" or "If I were to interview 10 people today all with the same qualifications on paper as you have, why should I hire you rather than one of the others?"

7. AVOID QUESTIONS THAT CAN BE ANSWERED WITH YES OR NO
   A question which requires an explanation or elaboration will elicit more information. For example, "Why did you leave school?" is much better than "Did you leave school to go to work?" The latter infers the type of answer you're seeking and it makes it extremely easy for the candidate to give you the response he thinks will please you. Use of the words "why," "how," "where," "when," "what," and "who" in phrasing help you avoid falling into the leading-question trap.

8. WHEN RESISTANCE OCCURS, PROBE FOR THE REASONS
   Occasionally, candidates will resist answering certain questions and become defensive. This could be due to any of several reasons. The information may discredit him or he might not fully understand the significance of the question. There are two good techniques for handling defensiveness:

A. Drop the question and come back to it when he or she is more open.

B. Explain that these questions are asked of each candidate because the information is necessary in making an effective decision.

9. CONTROL YOUR PERSONAL OPINIONS
The interview should not serve as a sounding board for your personal opinions and beliefs, nor should it be used to give advice, suggestions or criticisms. Whatever the candidate's response to a question, do not indicate concern or surprise, or express an opinion as to whether it's good or bad. If you do, you'll soon find the candidate giving you answers designed to please you rather than to inform.

10. RECORD ANSWERS AS YOU GET THEM
You can't possibly remember the answers to all the questions you'll ask. Therefore, it's essential to take notes as the interview proceeds. Experience has shown that very few candidates will object. In most cases the candidate will be impressed with your business-like manner, and flattered that you are recording his statements.

11. END THE INTERVIEW ON A FRIENDLY NOTE
It's important that you send each candidate away with a good feeling toward you and your school. Thank him or her for the time spent and the directness with which he or she has answered your questions. At the conclusion of the interview, ask to be excused for a few minutes. Then make your over-all evaluation of the interview and inform the candidate as to whether he or she is to be given further consideration. In any case, send the candidate away feeling that he or she has had a square deal.

4. COMPARE AND DECIDE

A. After you have narrowed the list to those applicants you would really consider, proceed with the following:

1. Check all personal references. Inquire about intelligence, problem-solving ability, common sense, personal-

ity, perserverance, stability, family compatibility, and so forth.

   2. Check business references, and promptness of payment.

   3. Check former employers; verify dates, salary. Inquire about ability, sociability, reason for leaving. Ask if they would re-hire.

   4. Verify attendance, diplomas, degrees at all schools listed.

B. Additional optional screening.

   1. Credit check is of particular importance if the job requires handling money.

   2. Testing - for intelligence, aptitude, ability.

   3. Home interview. To determine whether the candidate has the kind of home support and cooperation from the spouse and family that is essential to effective performance.

   4. Physical Examination. Particularly if there is any history of chronic illness.

C. Review your facts on each applicant. Compare what you should know on each applicant against the requirement of the job.

D. Compare candidate against candidate. Allow the supervisor who will oversee this worker to assist in the decision if you are in doubt. Choose the best person for the job.

Chapter 5

Keeping Staff Morale High

To have a job we like is certainly one of the pleasures in life. Enjoying one's work, however, does not depend solely on an aptitude for the work performed. Much of our esteem for our jobs depends on the personalities of others with whom we work.

To rub elbows with a malcontent for eight hours can turn anyone of us into a clock watcher. The job we once arrived early for becomes one big drag. We roll over when the alarm goes off delaying as long as we can, and the ride in is filled with thoughts of "There must be a better way to make a living." We blame others for our mood—and yet in answer to the first "Good morning" thrown our way, we respond with a spontaneous "What's good about it?"

If we are to teach, really teach, we must set an example, knowing full well that much of the success of our students will depend on their positive, happy attitudes. It is absurd to think we can stand before a class and command; "You are to smile and be happy, or else!" If every member of your staff is not pleased to be with you, assisting to maintain an exuberant school personality, effect change or say goodbye. Causing change is not as difficult as you may think, if we simply revert to the three basic rules for handling people:

1. Never nag, hassle, argue or complain.
2. Offer praise, recognition and hope.
3. Make other people want to do things.

The boss naturally has the responsibility of creating the total atmosphere, but each employee, being aware of the fact he or she must determine his or her own destiny, can also assume this responsibility. Those who can spread sunshine can expect to be rewarded, particularly if they can influence those living in a permanent eclipse.

Even if that guy who signs the paychecks is "top grouch," he is not blind to the value of Sunshine Spreaders. They are often first in line at the bonus window.

Many years ago, I read a poem by John Milton that seems appropriate here and I'd like to share it with you. It is titled "The Inner Light":

He that has light within his own clear breast
May sit in the center of the Earth and enjoy bright day:
But he that hides a dark soul and foul thoughts
Benighted walks under the midday sun
Himself, his own dungeon.

To me this was one more revelation that we alone create our own despair or our own exhilaration. We can assist others to come to this conclusion through a contagious reaction if we develop our own plan. Here are a few suggestions:

A) Don't allow yourself to think negatively. If you do, you can't help but be a complainer.

B) Always smile and offer a friendly greeting.

C) Show concern about any occurrences in the private lives of those you meet. Offer praise and recognition for accomplishment or good fortune. Offer sympathy, understanding and hope for those with problems.

D) Offer to assist when you can.

E) Be constantly aware of work done well. Let others know you noticed.

   1. Awards can be a fine motivator, when it is clear to all how the winner is chosen. By that, I mean one person's opinion should never be the basis for an award. This simply causes animosity, as most of the others involved may feel they were equally or more deserving.

      At Lincoln Technical Institute in Dallas, director Julius Fambry has come up with a formula for choosing an "Instructor of the Phase" award that looks like a good one. The award is based on 3 factors:

      a. OVERALL CLASS ATTENDANCE. Figured by: Total sessions minus absences divided by total sessions equals percentage.

      b. INTERRUPTIONS DURING THE PHASE. Figured by: Total students starting the phase minus interrupts during the phase divided by total students starting the phase equals percentage.

      c. INTERRUPTS AT THE END OF THE PHASE. Figured by: Net students after interruptions (from b above) minus interruptions at the end of the phase divided by net students equals percentage.

      The instructor with the best combined percentage wins the award. This, of course, is simply figured by adding the a,b,c percentages and dividing by 3.

   2. A handwritten note on a pay stub.

   3. Cards on birthdays, anniversaries, or no special day at all.

   4. Give an employee extra money in cash for a specific purpose, for example: "I'd like you to take your wife out to dinner on us."

5. Similarly give tickets to plays, concerts, or sporting events.

6. Send flowers, cards, or humorous items when employees are out due to illness.

7. Give time off not to be counted as vacation.

F) Show respect for others by making them feel important:

1. Listen to suggestions and try to implement all or part of the idea. Even if the idea seems stupid or old hat, listen and show your appreciation. Thank the person for his concern and tell him or her you will consider it.

2. Solicit their opinion. Often this can result in productivity that otherwise would not have happened. People are more anxious to implement their own ideas. Not too long ago I did a favor for a capable employee by hiring an unskilled brother-in-law wanted by no one else. It was no wonder. Despite an explicit written list of his duties as a maintenance man, he neglected tasks with the ease of a man who had a great deal of experience. The outstanding example of his negligence was a restroom in a wing of our main building. My disgust with the condition of this room was so great that had I not had access to another facility of identical function, I might have expired of kidney disorder. My patience exhausted, I summoned the employee to my office. Fortunately he took so long to appear that I had time to think. Otherwise, I'm sure I would have offered some spontaneous emotional remarks that would have resulted in filling out the forms for unemployment compensation within 48 hours.

I said to Jerry: "I can't figure out a way to solve a problem that is driving me crazy. If you can come up with an answer I'd be willing to fill up your gas tank the next time it's bone dry!" I got his attention. I then went on to describe how the students were reckless in their use of the bathroom in question and because there was not time during classes to clean, the Board of Health might walk in and levy a fine or take us to court.

Jerry agreed it was a problem and walked out. Within ten minutes he was back to see me. "I've got an idea!" he said. "If I come in at 7 a.m. instead of 8 I can catch that room before morning class." "Why didn't I think of that." I responded. I went on to say how brilliant he was. From that day on, you could have held a Bar Mitzvah in that room at any time with complete confidence. It was the cheapest tank of gas I ever bought.

G) Provide the means by which closely-related categories of employees can work together for a common objective.

1. If our instructors as a group are graded by our students at an average of 95% or above, at the end of the phase of training they go to a luncheon bought by management. Incidentally, we by no means restrict their appetites at these events. Fancy hor d'oeuvres to elaborate desserts are the order of the day. And this is the way we want it. Something special to look forward to!

2. The office staff similarly can go to lunch if the accounts receivable balance at the end of the month.

3. At the Connecticut Business Institute in Stratford, president Emanuel Pallant came up with a novel way of thanking his staff for reduced attrition. Working with his known rate of 12% attrition he offered 20% of the tuition savings for any drop in the rate, and an additional 35% if the overall attrition rate dropped below 9%. The money is put into a kitty for all to share. After five months the dropout rate fell below 10%.

H) Plan company get-togethers, but don't be responsible for creating familiarity that may cause domestic problems.

1. Picnics, parties, theatre trips and the like. Always include spouses and dates. Discourage singles from attending unless you are confident no triangles can result.

2. Bowling, golf and other tournaments. Okay 'for employees only,' but schedule wisely.

3. Open Houses, student dances, promotional dinners, and other extracurricular school activities. Form committees. Create a little friendly competition. Treat all participants to meals and extras. Don't pay overtime; work with volunteers only, but make sure they enjoy themselves.

I) Plan gifts for special occasions. Even some that aren't so special.

Every job at times can get a little monotonous, just as all of us occasionally get the idea we aren't appreciated for what we do. Smart employers (smart husbands and wives, too) can get a lot of mileage out of a small gift when given in appreciation, particularly if a personal note is attached. There's something about getting an unexpected tribute, regardless of the monetary value, that makes it significant. Such thoughtfulness can promote an uncommon allegiance, if not given as a matter of policy or tradition.

About the only time our staff expects something now is for Easter, Thanksgiving and Christmas, but they don't know what it will be. On just about any other day I may or may not give something. Ground Hog Day is among my favorites. Gifts have included hams, cheese, turkeys, steaks, crockery, glass, small kitchen appliances, candy, books, jewelry and a myriad of nonsensical items. You might consider free vitamins, flu shots, ethnic luncheons, free coffee days, pizza meetings, raffles of items received as payola, football pools, etc. And even for the kids of your staff: Easter and Christmas parties and pet shows.

J) Keep your communication open.

1. Provide an opportunity for everyone to voice an opinion before major decisions are made which may affect their lives. Depending on the nature of the question, consider private and individual conversations rather than staff

meetings. Chances are you will unearth more deep-seated opinions than you will in an open meeting.

2. If you hold staff meetings, have specific dates and times designated well in advance. Impromptu decisions by management can be a source of irritation for employees who have planned their time.

3. Depending on the size of your school, establish a company newsletter. Use it to motivate and to encourage further motivation.

Now we have made a few suggestions as to how to raise morale, a few words on what not to do. Whereas building morale can be a slow and tedious task, destroying it can take less time than it took you to dispose of your last paycheck.

A) Be cordial, but by no means overly familiar with your employees. Ignore this advice and you'll find the old cliche about breeding contempt to be quite accurate.

B) Avoid having employees' salaries known to all. Envy is a costly problem; every one of us has a way to justify that he or she should be paid as well, if not better than someone else. Unfortunately, we are not capable of seeing ourselves as others see us. Consequently, none of us can assess our own values. Few employees can accept that their employer's judgement may be accurate.

Move payroll outside your organization if at all possible. When hiring a new employee, have it understood that salaries are to be kept confidential. Every time a raise is given, reiterate this policy.

C) Don't live with a rabble-rouser. Regardless of his or her position, regardless if compensation must be paid, find a way to promptly say goodbye. Having a happy progressive staff is essential to sound education, and it only takes one chronic complainer to turn the mood of your staff upside down. If this is the case, consider unemployment compensation as a wise investment!

Chapter 6

Creating A Home Away From Home

When I was an advertising salesman years ago I called regularly on a woman's shoe store that unmistakably appealed to those who were willing to pay a little more. Of course, no signs were hanging in the window that told you this. You simply got the idea when you walked in the door: the plush carpet, the magnificent decor, the elaborate furniture and the tailored suits worn by the salesman all shouted the message, "You're going to pay more!"

Their marketing didn't stop with just what the eyes could behold, however. The salesman gave personalized attention, recognizing every woman's foot as that which could have fit the glass slipper.

Despite all this, and with more than an adequate clientele, profits were little better than pathetic.

Management checked mark-up, buying patterns, and overhead. Everything appeared to be in line. No one could figure out what the problem was. No one except the kid who came in at closing time to clean up. As he was instructed to wait until all the customers left before operating the vaccum cleaner, he was fully aware of the problem: "Well if you ask me it's 'cause these women spend so damn much time making up their minds!" He hit the nail on the head.

Management had successfully created an inviting atmosphere to get women to come in and be treated royally. They hadn't considered how difficult it would be to get them to make a decision and leave.

After considering everything from insults to parking meters, they stumbled on the answer. They consulted a color psychologist who advised them to paint the walls a certain shade of pink and then cover it with an intricate design.

The idea was to maintain the elaborate decor, while subconsciously irritating those who sat and looked at it for any length of time. This worked. The duration of the average sale was reduced by twenty minutes. Profits improved by over 30% and the customers were just as pleased, being unaware of the reason for their impatience.

So whether you know it or not - your decor could be keeping or losing students.

The atmosphere at your school should be carefully considered so as to blend with the type and age group of your students. Color, furnishings, illustrations, lighting, carpeting, signs, bulletin boards, printed material, food, snacks, odors, seating, lounges, maintenance, and music should be well thought out and researched.

Over the years, I have visited many schools throughout the country which had predominant color schemes of battleship grey, mildew green or dungeon brown. Frankly I never understood why, but in each case I had the overwhelming feeling that if I were in attendance there I wouldn't have the option of leaving voluntarily. I'd have to escape! Demoralizing? You said it, and the results showed on the unsmiling faces of the student body.

To create a new, lively, more desirable atmosphere at your school, start with elbow grease and paint. It's a small investment that could pay big dividends, particularly if you were to have a contest, offering cash awards to the class judged to have done the best job with their classroom.

Color is just one item to be considered. Red Voldness, a multiple school owner in Ohio, offers this sage advice;

"When I first go into a school, I will improve everything that touches the senses of the student. The place must look good, smell good, feel good, and sound good, and the food, though a necessary evil, must taste good."

As an abstract goal, you might keep in mind that you intend to create an environment that is more hospitable than the average student's home. This is of particular importance for those schools that provide housing. The idea of living in a cell is not conducive to a favorable learning environment.

Of primary importance, once your "Show Place" has been created, is keeping it in exemplary condition. Many schoolowners have told me: "What's the use of dressing up the place, it will only look like hell in a few days anyway!" Not so, if you don't let it happen. Consider the following suggestions:

1. In your orientations, challenge each new student with the responsibility of upholding the image of the school. Point out that visiting employers who may someday hire them must be impressed with the appearance of the school. Sell Pride.

2. Establish a systematic and thorough program of maintenance and repair.

3. Make students aware of the fact they must clean up their own work areas. Tying in dismissal with having every one's work area in shape can make peer pressure work in your favor.

4. Anytime that you discover student negligence or an intentional defacing of the premises (such as graffiti in the rest rooms) stop all classes that utilize the area defaced, and hold a mass meeting of all students. Point out that such damage leads to higher tuition rates in addition to creating an immature reputation that may well dissuade a potential employer from hiring your graduates. In short, that all negligence costs each student money.

By immediately letting students know that you consider such acts outrageous, you will see a very positive reaction. To allow negligent acts to go on without sounding an alarm is like thinking, "Well, it's only a little hole in the dike!"

It is stretching the imagination to believe that anyone would drop out of school because of housekeeping or dull surroundings, but to the Felix Ungers of the world it could be a strong contributing factor. Anyway you look at it, your environment is important.

Speaking of environment, you should also look into other areas of human behavior that you might assume are of little concern. To a few, they could be traumatic.

1. Language. Don't allow your staff to indulge in profanity, vulgarity or dirty jokes. Keep your education clean and professional. Similarly reprimand students who have careless tongues. The logic behind your argument is just this; good use of the English language offends no one. Poor use of the language will offend many. Customers, bosses, and other influential people may all silently avoid you, seldom saying why. It can cost you plenty in the form of jobs, raises, commission and good friends. This is the price of ignorance. Chances are ironically that you'll cuss out others for not giving you the breaks.

2. Smoking. No longer acceptable to many and the voices of the nonsmoker are getting louder. If smoking is allowed in your classrooms, make sure of adequate ventilation and provide "no smoking" sections. On the other hand a "no smoking anywhere" policy is not advisable. Arrange times and places so that nicotine fits are avoidable. The avid smoker will take a walk, too, if he feels management is unreasonable.

3. Drugs, Alcohol, Fighting. You are better off making it well known that violators will be promptly suspended and you make no exceptions. A slap on the wrist is hardly sufficient. Such action will only have observers take tales home to moms and pops who could well decide your school doesn't possess the environment they want their kid brought up in.

In short, the environment you fashion should be based on prevailing common sense. It should be in writing and no employee or student should spend his or her first day without receiving a full explanation of the whys and wherefores.

Chapter 7

Know
Your Attrition Rates

It is a fact that to succeed at anything a thought-out plan is advisable, almost essential. Yet to establish a goal to reduce attrition is hardly feasible unless we know where we are and where we hope to go.

Honesty is important in compiling these statistics. Over the years I have seen an unbelievable number of ways to calculate attrition. Many serve to pay tribute to the ingenuity of their authors but otherwise are of little significance.

Anyone who really seeks to reduce attrition should not be ashamed of the rate compiled. Playing with statistics is not among the answers to the problem, and it won't save you a dime.

The variables that often confuse us are: length of course, those interrupting and re-entering, students attending beyond their original date of graduation, the actual date of interruption, and the mathematics involved.

The best way to obtain accurate records on attrition and retention is to trace all students from the day they start school to the day they leave.

Unfortunately, this often takes a great amount of time beyond the original graduation date. Consequently, your current efforts are difficult to assess on courses of any length.

To get a figure that offers an adequate basis for comparison you might consider the following three-step formula. Many schools now do this monthly and after 12 months or the duration of either a semester or a school year are able to calculate accurate statistics.

STEP 1 —Total population at beginning of period plus new students added during the period = Total

STEP 2 —Total interrupted enrollments during the period minus re-entered students during the period = Net loss due to interruption.

STEP 3 —Divide the net loss due to interruption (Step 2) by the total from Step 1 to get your attrition percentage.

    To make sure your figures are accurate you can take the total from Step 1, deduct the total from Step 2, then deduct the total graduates during the same period. The result should equal the total students in attendance at the end of the period.

As your attrition figures will often vary greatly from one course to another, it is wise to utilize the above process for each individual course, night and day. This will more distinctly indicate your problem areas.

You can then use all your totals to come up with your institutional attrition and retention rates, but in reality these are not as indicative as your specific course totals.

Chapter 8

Recruiting With Dropouts In Mind

As I researched opinions for this book, no cure for attrition was more frequently cited than: "A good recruitment procedure." Leo de Gar Kulka, president of the College for Recording Arts in San Francisco, put it this way: "Reduced attrition starts with factual and realistic advertising and recruitment."

Very seldom do we think of our advertising as a cause of attrition but it certainly can be. Being proud of our schools, we or our ad agencies can become overly zealous in describing what we have to offer. It may provide an honest picture of how we view ourselves. On the other hand, the prospect has a different perspective. Before putting your ideas into any medium it is a sound idea to have uninvolved observers give their opinions.

If you have ever had children reach their senior year in high school then you are probably familiar with the volume of mail they receive relevant to furthering their education. Frankly, I was astounded. For 3 years we actually got more ads than bills.

Now, if you don't have a senior coming up this year at your house, I suggest you find one in your neighborhood. Then ask him or her to save all the direct mail received so that you can examine it. This is an education you shouldn't pass up.

Any way you do it, you'll find this material revealing. Many schools portray their offerings as though gaining an education is comparable to a Caribbean cruise. Even the U.S. Army uses sex, travel and adventure as a lure. It's sad.

How many disillusioned students have dropped out when faced with the reality is anybody's guess. If it's happened to you, I sincerely hope it wasn't intentional. To make sure it doesn't happen to you, simply remember to "tell it like it is."

Julius Brenner, the hardworking president of the Ohio Diesel Technical Institute in Cleveland, offered some observations about school catalogs that hit the nail on the head: "The catalog that addresses itself to a variety of veiled untruths or wispy training promises will add to the discovery of empty classroom seats. We must ask: Is it honest in its description of the training curriculum? Do photographs portray actual and operational facilities and equipment? When a reference is made to 'hands on', 'practical', or 'industry oriented training', is such comment honest and factual? Failures and omissions within the catalog become a most important contributing factor to student departures."

Just as you must monitor your advertising you must know what your sales representatives are telling students. You must also be aware of what they are not telling students!

In either case it is best to establish a "second interview procedure" in which a salaried employee other than a salesman goes over every aspect of your school so that future misunderstandings can be avoided. It's not a bad idea, either, to have a new enrollee sign a paper which details the points discussed.

An analysis made at the Elmira Business Institute in Elmira, New York gives ample reason to conclude that we should never take short-cuts in our enrollment procedure. John Hyland, it's director, says: "We found that the student rushed through the admissions procedure at the eleventh hour is often the one to appear on the attrition list."

The message seems clear. Take the time to be thorough and agonizingly factual. The benefits of such an approach were described in a letter received from D.E. Shollenberger, director of the Welder Training Testing Institute in Cornwell Heights, Pennsylvania. I find it worthy of reprinting in full.

Dear Mr. Diggs:

We at W.T.T.I. have suffered along with every other school when it came to student dropouts; we no longer do!

Let me give you a little background, and explain what we did to correct this problem.

Several years ago we had an admission staff made up of professional school recruiters. Men were paid on a commission basis for each enrollment attained with a requirement the student completes five weeks or more before the commission was earned. Our thinking was if they stayed the first month our program was dynamic enough to keep them - wrong! Our two schools were full, but the "back door" stayed open.

After several years, the administration took a long look at our admissions policies, admissions staff, and most of all student files of those who dropped out. After discussions with some of the students who did drop out, it was obvious that they were not deceived by the admissions staff, but they were not told all of the facts about welding, such as conditions, environment, tough trade, etc. We then released our admissions staff. From that day, all admissions were taken over by myself and another member of my staff. We reviewed our admissions policy and added only one thing: a "black list." This list told everything we knew to be bad about the field the student was about to enter. We told them it was hot-cold inside work, outside work, heavy lifting, smokey, and at times dangerous. We told them they would be called upon to weld on their backs, knees, and on ladders/scaffolds, or just by hanging on with one hand while welding with the other. Our enrollment dropped at an alarming rate and we were concerned, but we were sure we had chosen the right way. We would stick it out and give our rebuilding program a chance.

The results after a number of months were dramatic.

We had less:
(A) student problems (drugs, fights, etc.)
(B) loss of time by the student
(C) loss of equipment
(D) DROPOUTS (amazing)

We had:
(A) interested students
(B) better attendance
(C) better placement percentages
(D) satisfied agencies and employers
(E) students who completed all of their courses and were representing the school in the highest manner

One very important point; we DID NOT change anything else in the school. We just dropped admissions staff and added the black list. We found you must tell it like it really is, no matter how bad things may appear to be. If you tell the prospective student up-front it's a busy tough trade and that he may not like it, you will lose the candidate who is "shopping" for a salary or position. But, you will retain the truly interested candidate because he knows he's been told the "whole" truth. I've found most of those candidates did previous investigations into the career and sometimes the school, even before they visited us.

Today, Mr. Diggs, we employ a salaried director of admissions who has a degree and no prior proprietary trade school experience. I personally trained him for one month in what I wanted said to each candidate. Along with my training he was required to take one of our welder training courses (on his own time) and now he is better informed about the trade. I personally orient each class to re-emphasize the "black list" and I make it a point to get into the classroom at least two or three times more during their stay with us. I confront all problems as they develop and not hope they will go away. Once again, our two schools are near capacity and we are considering an expansion program. Mr. Diggs, very few schools would do what we did. We were only able to do this on the strength of our staff; and with everyone, and I mean everyone feeling the pinch, no one quit. But we are now able to do more for our staff and intend to do more next year.

Today our attrition rate is under 10% and we have had months where we did not lose a student, for any reason. If we do lose a student it's either for financial reasons or family problems. In most cases we are the ones who "drop" the student for poor attendance or performance.

In summary, the only solution to keeping that back door closed is what is done at the front door. We found our key and have been satisfied since. I hope other school directors can be as lucky.

Regards,

D.E. Schollenberger
Administrator

ABOUT TESTING

Personally, I feel there is value in tests that measure both aptitude and intelligence. Neither high school diplomas nor transcripts can provide the indication of what can be expected as does a test with which we have become acquainted.

This point was made clear in a letter from the Skadron College of Business in San Bernardino. "Over the past 10 years we have developed our own entrance test that has a minimum cut-off score for acceptance into the college and is also used for diagnostic work. Presently we have to reject approximately 25% of the graduating seniors from California high schools because they can't handle our easiest program."

Many schools today, unfortunately, don't use testing in their enrollment process, and they say: "We can't find one that is appropriate for us."

That being the case, I would suggest you develop your own as did Skadron College. For that matter, it doesn't even have to be a written exam.

The A.T.E.S. Technical School in Ohio has used a testing procedure for over 20 years. Applicants are invited to attend a session which includes a lecture and demonstration followed by a "hands on" project and an evaluation. Both the school and student gain a pretty good idea as to whether the student is suited for the course.

Advocates of open enrollment policies generally feel that because a student has the desire to pursue a particular career he should be allowed to do so. After all, what's more important than wanting something when considering the prerequisites for success? A good point, certainly with much validity, but not altogether conclusive.

Our goals in life must be realistic in every detail. A fifty year old man has little chance today of starting an ambitious program at the local playground with the ultimate objective of playing shortstop for the New York Yankees. Similarly, a woman with five small children might find her goal of peace by deciding to desert her family to join the convent.

All of us have visualized objectives and wished we could be somebody or somewhere or have something. Perhaps we have even made impulsive decisions to start to achieve the goals, only to find that down the road there were a number of detours that made the journey no longer worthwhile. Sure, we might like to arrive at the goal we have visualized; but the getting there must be examined realistically.

A good example might be that experienced at any Auto Mechanics School. Almost every day a few women will inquire about enrollment, motivated by such reasons as: "I'm tired of getting ripped off by male chauvinists", "I want to make better wages than I now make in the office", "My boyfriend likes girls who know about cars", "My husband dared me!"

With the "Open Enrollment" policy, most of these women could be added to your enrollment list, but almost certainly would also be added to your attrition list.

Applicants must see the Career for what it really is. As for being an auto mechanic, it means almost always having cut and leather-like hands, with grease under any fingernail you might have left. It means lifting, pulling, pushing, stretching, while oil, sludge, salt, and whatever falls in your hair and your face and saturates your clothes. It means working in extreme heat and extreme cold, often in positions which the human body was not meant to get into.

I personally believe that "Open Admission" policies can not lead to long term stability. They may be a quick fix for your profit picture, but over a period of years, they very easily could cause a downward spiral of profits which cannot be stopped. Here are my reasons for feeling as I do:

A) To appeal to your "average" student you will have to adjust the level of your education downward. You will cover less material in any given period of time.

B) Your more intelligent students will be bored, and not being challenged, will often drop out.

C) Despite establishing a lower standard of achievement, those who do not possess an aptitude for the subject matter will still drop out.

D) The reputation you will gain as "Easy" and "for dummies" will dissuade many good students from enrolling.

E) This "negative image" will gradually spread to those who could hire your graduates but they will hesitate to do so. A diploma from a school that is "a joke within the industry" can be worse that none at all!

F) Poor placement means few, if any, referrals, high drop out rates, and ever escalating default rates.

If you have a sincere desire to help those who can't pass an entrance test that will assure applicants can benefit, then consider setting up remedial courses as prerequisites to your regular fare. By no means lessen the quality of the education you offer. It could very well be an irreversible error in judgement.

The Teterboro School of Aeronautics in New Jersey has a worthwhile procedure. In addition to requiring that applicants return for a second interview accompanied by parents, fiances, or spouses, they are taken for a tour of airport facilities that employ mechanics. The prospect subsequently has a clear idea of both learning and working.

The folks at Cleveland's West Side Institute of Technology don't tour facilities where their graduates might work, but they use another twist to the second-interview technique. Each Saturday they hold an open house to which all prospective students and their families are invited. Faculty and staff members meet with the prospects in a very informal setting. Everyone is introduced and a hot lunch is served. Dick Pountney, the president, whom I personally know to have one of the biggest hearts in the field of education, says: "We talk about what was, what is, and what can be. And somehow this works!"

FINANCING TUITION

This subject has much to do with your attrition rate and probably for more reasons than you've considered. For both under-financing and over-financing can provide innumerable reasons to buy Excedrin by the case.

A thorough knowledge of federal programs by at least one member of your staff is essential. But by itself this hardly provides a financial aid department of maximum effectiveness.

Your student financial aid officer should:

a) be aware of all current financial aid programs whether or not you utilize all of them.

b) schedule the payment of benefits so the student is not awarded large sums of money which could be disposed of for purposes unrelated to his education.

c) develop a sound, workable program with your placement director to provide part-time jobs.

d) be familiar with a system of budgeting which can be advocated to the student prior to commencement of classes.

e) be thoroughly acquainted with your school's own financing, so that money is available whenever weekly, monthly, quarterly, semester, or term tuition is due.

Let's elaborate on these one at a time and see how they apply to your school.

A. Know all Federal Aid Programs. To some it may seem stupid to study those programs you don't utilize, but it makes sense for several reasons. 1. Competition: "You had better keep up with the Joneses." 2. To provide answers to those prospects who want to know why you don't participate in a specific program. 3. To know if you can utilize a program when the prerequistes for participation are altered. 4. So you might better comprehend the advantages and disadvantages of altering your courses, starting new courses, or changing your corporate structure.

B. For many young men and women, large sums of money cannot be handled and become a temptation. They gain the perspective of the average embezzler: " I'll just use it for a while and pay it back later." "After all, cheating the government is okay as long as your not caught!" "Nobody is paying back these loans anyway!"

Unless your school controls the disbursement of loan and grant funds you are inviting students to take the money and run. We think it is wise to have all checks sent to the school; yes, V.A. checks too. Then be firm in your requests to have the entire amount applied to the student's account, if not current.

Many schools use SEOG and PELL funds to insure better attendance. Checks are written either weekly or bi-weekly. This is particularly good advice for rehabilitation and JTPA students whose tuition is paid. No school, no pay!

C. Use of effective part-time job placement is important and often essential for many students who don't qualify for or have enough personal financial assistance to make it through their chosen course.

The key to utilizing placement as a means to prolong student attendance is to have highly skilled placement people. They must make employers understand that student workers should stay with their education, and that changing hours, shifts or duties that might interfere with class hours or homework cannot be condoned.

D. Many students unfortunately drop for financial reasons even though their credit analysis at the time of enrollment indicated no apparent problems. The reason, for the most part, is the acquisition of debt after acceptance. Sound budgeting advice at the time of the second interview is not a bad idea.

For a free copy of a budget book you can use to counsel students, just drop a line to:

>Progressive Publications
>P.O. Box 4016
>Homosassa Springs, Florida 32647

E. As it is unintelligent to become heavily dependent on federal or state aid, take the time to sit down and ask yourself how you could survive without the assistance of government.
You may find that you can do more with your own financing ingenuity than you first think.

Chapter 9

Being Aware of Potential Dropouts

For a major-league pitcher to rise to the top of his profession, it's almost essential that he study the record of each batter he is going to pitch to in his next outing. He's got to know every man's strengths and weaknesses in addition to what he has been doing at the plate recently. Failure to do this results in an early shower.

On the other hand, the batting coach must be similarly knowledgeable so as to work on the weaknesses and correct them. The school owner must play the role of the coach–hopefully preparing each student for the Big Leagues when they leave your institution with diploma in hand.

If you intend to do the most with each student, you sure can't funnel everyone through the same machinery and expect uniform results. No more than the batting coach who insists on one stance and one arc to the swing.

Gathering the information necessary to counsel effectively is worth several times more than a pound of cure. This can best be accomplished in a second interview by the individual or individuals who perform your student counseling.

With a copy of the form in front of you that appears on the next page, determine through the information already provided and further questioning just where the applicant could use help.

Taking each category let's explore the questions we might ask to come to a conclusion.

1. HISTORY OF PERSISTANCE

a) Did the applicant finish high school or other postsecondary schools attended?

b) If not, why not?

c) Has the applicant a history of holding jobs for short periods only?

d) If so, why?

2. READING COMPREHENSION

a) Does the applicant like to read?

b) If we were to provide supplemental training in reading improvement would the student attend?

3. MATHEMATICS
(if this is important to the career sought)

a) Did the applicant have difficulty with math in the past?

b) If we were to provide supplemental training in math, would the student attend?

4. APTITUDE

a) Why does the applicant believe he or she would be happy working in the career chosen?

b) Has the applicant had any previous experience (at school, at work, with organizations, etc.) that would indicate an aptitude for the chosen career?

INDIVIDUAL'S NAME:	SHOULD BE SATISFACTORY FOR COMPLETION	NEEDS SOME IMPROVEMENT	HAS A SERIOUS PROBLEM	REMAINS DOUBTFUL	SUGGESTIONS:
History of persistence with education and/or employment					
Reading comprehension					
Mathematics					
Aptitude					
Student's chances of being socially accepted					
Close family ties					
Prior acceptance of discipline					
Home and personal life styles					
Current emotional problems (Divorce, Job, etc.)					
Health					
Finances sufficient through duration of training					
Specific objective in mind to utilize training					
Family and friends who share prospects objectives					
Self-sufficiency as the result of relocation					
Professed desire					
Availability of sufficient time for classes and study					

5. SOCIAL ACCEPTABILITY

a) Does the applicant have any religious beliefs which would make it difficult for him or her to survive in your school environment?

b) Is the applicant self-conscious or have any physical or mental hang-ups?

c) Does the applicant have any obvious racial or religious prejudices?

d) Are there any characteristics such as language, dress, grooming, etc., which could result in embarrassment for the applicant or others?

6. CLOSE FAMILY TIES

a) Does the applicant maintain that he or she has a healthy relationship with parents, sisters, brothers, wife?

7. PRIOR ACCEPTANCE OF DISCIPLINE

a) Is there any indication in the applicant's background to indicate that he or she has difficulty accepting rules and regulations?

8. HOME AND PERSONAL LIFE STYLES

a) Is the professed social life of the applicant apt to interfere with satisfactory progress?

b) What are the applicant's TV watching habits?

c) Does the applicant have any avocations, hobbies, or habits that could interfere with getting sufficient sleep—or getting to school everyday and on time?

9. CURRENT EMOTIONAL PROBLEMS

a) Is the applicant currently under a strain as the result of divorce proceedings, and upcoming trial, sickness or death in the family, etc.?

10. HEALTH

a) Are there any chronic or spasmodic conditions that could result in interruption of schooling?

11. FINANCES

a) Does the applicant thoroughly understand what funds are forthcoming, how they will be received, how they are to be applied to the account, what the terms are for repayment of loans, etc.?

b) Does the applicant currently have the funds available to pay the tuition through the duration of his course–or is he or she dependent on future employment or some other means of obtaining funds in the future?

c) If the applicant's finances are questionable, has he or she explored the possibility of loans and grants from all sources?

12. SPECIFIC CAREER OBJECTIVES

a) Does the applicant have a specific career objective in mind at the conclusion of training?

13. FAMILY AND FRIENDS WHO SHARE THE PROSPECT'S OBJECTIVES

a) Is there anyone closely associated with the applicant who opposes the idea of pursuing this career?

b) Do those closely associated with the applicant support his or her career choice, and will they encourage the applicant to succeed?

14. SELF-SUFFICIENCY OF THOSE RELOCATING

   a) Has the applicant lined up housing with which he or she is pleased?

   b) Does the applicant have friends or a roommate to associate with?

   c) Does the applicant miss his or her family, friends, etc., to the degree that it is a good possibility he or she will return home before finishing?

15. PROFESSED DESIRE

   a) Is the applicant convinced that this is undoubtedly the field he or she wants?

   b) Does the applicant profess a strong desire to complete this program?

16. AVAILABILITY OF SUFFICIENT TIME FOR CLASSES AND STUDY

   a) Does the applicant currently work hours that necessitate getting little sleep or sleeping on a split shift?

   b) Does the applicant have other obligations which will make it difficult to study, do homework assignments and/or attend classes regularly?

After working with this checklist for a while, an experienced counselor will be able to detect areas of concern and to schedule counseling sessions accordingly. Prevention is the objective.

If you do not provide the extra assistance which so many students need today, you can pretty much expect your school to stay in the minor leagues.

Chapter 10

Preventing Cancellations And No Shows

For some reason the average student recruiter thinks his effort ends with the applicant's signature on a contract.

An understandable parallel is the groom who no longer deals in flowers, candy, poems, cards and what have you, once he has combed the rice out of his hair. Divorce is often the abrupt response of the disillusioned bride. And of course this same situation works in reverse. Either way the marriage never gets off the ground.

As discussed previously, "telling it like it is" is of primary importance, but that is not all. The applicant cannot be left with the idea that once he has paid his money and signed his name, the courtship is over.

The days immediately following enrollment are the most critical whether you enroll in the school or in the home. This is the time when the applicant divulges to those in his environment what he plans to do and in so doing gathers numerous unsolicited opinions, many of which are often the negative conclusions of those who claim to know better.

Think back to when you last made a major purchase. How many people said to you, "Gee, I wish I had known, I could have gotten you a better deal."

Among the common arguments the applicant may listen to are: "Private trade schools are all crooked!" "You can get the same education at the community college for a fraction of the cost!" "Listen kid, I'll give you a job and teach you the trade besides!" And very often: "You are capable of doing much better than going into that trade!"

Along with the doubts conjured up by others, the applicant may come up with plenty of his own: Can I handle school after a long absence from the classroom? Can I fit in with others? Can I relocate and live with others? Can I work and study too? Is the school really good? Will I be ready to work in this occupation upon graduation?

So as to keep the applicant sold, it is important that we schedule and continue our efforts up to the first day of class, for cancellations and no shows are often related to the length of time between enrollment and starting class. No applicant should be allowed to lose sight of the future nor the benefits of the unique and specialized training you offer. Here are some suggestions:

1. Send an immediate "Thank you from the director" letter. Assure the enrollee that he or she has made a wise decision. Encourage the student to call if any questions arise. And type the letter individually. Form letters don't do much to convince the recipient you really care.

2. Send an immediate letter to those who provide the home environment of the enrollee. This letter serves two purposes: to seriously solicit parents, spouses, and friends requesting their help in motivating the enrollee; and to convince these people that the enrollee has made a wise decision.
A sample of such a letter appears on the next page.

3. Follow up with regular, planned mailings and phone calls to the enrollee. Use the mail for:

a) Newsletters.

b) Articles about the school that have recently appeared in print.

c) Current employment statistics and placement data, including a list of recent employers.

d) Announcements of open houses, orientations, or other special events.

To those close to John Doe:

In the near future classes will start for John Doe that could well alter the course of his life. If completed successfully, they will lead to many fine opportunities. Unfortunately though, they are difficult, for we are fussy when it comes to handing out diplomas. Our graduates must know what they are doing. What you will find encouraging is that we tested John before we accepted him and we know he possesses the aptitude and intelligence to succeed.

The difference between those who make it and those who don't, however, is usually not intelligence. More often it is attitude, the ability to persevere when the going gets tough. This is why we are writing to you today. To ask you to help John complete this program.

Certainly, the saddest thing in the life of an educator is to see students give up who could definitely make it, simply because they lack confidence in themselves. So very often you see them a few years later working at a job that pays minimum wage, or worse yet, a job they simply can't stand, but must work because they need the money.

The future for a man or woman who knows mechanics offers a multitude of opportunities. Your support and encouragement can make the difference between obtaining them or falling short. Here, specifically, are a few things you can do:

1. Help this student to realize that the months of schooling ahead are a time of sacrifice and hard work and that the better jobs go to those who are better prepared. Urge him to be the best!

2. Make the student realize that personal habits like going out every night or being a TV addict must be adjusted. Sufficient sleep, time to study, good health, and self-discipline are an essential part of a new life style.

3. Encourage the student to establish a perfect attendance record, never absent, never late. Remind him that when it comes time to apply for the better jobs the discerning employer will look at the attendance record, considering it one of the most important of the requirements.

4. Caution the student about unnecessary purchases that could ultimately cause financial problems and interruption of schooling. Sure we'd all like to have a newer car or a better stereo, but there's a time and place for everything. An investment in education can never rust-out or be repossessed. And it can bring dividends that surpass those of any other investment made in a lifetime.

5. Assure the student that if he has difficulty with a technical or a personal problem we are here to help. Encourage him to speak up. We say in our publicity that "We care" about each student we accept. This is not just so much baloney. But to assist each student, open communication is a must. Sure, we'll sometimes suggest solutions that the student doesn't want to hear, but you may be assured that we firmly believe the answers provided will best serve the needs of the individual.

In summary, we are saying that, together, we can motivate this student to reach the utmost of his potential. It is important that we do so without nagging or hassling, however. We believe that training should be a pleasant and invigorating experience, and this can best be accomplished with love, understanding and constant encouragement.

If you'd care to know more about us, please accept our invitation to attend the orientation session to be held at the school on

On behalf of the entire staff I sincerely want to thank you for your interest and consideration.

> Respectfully,
>
> (your name)
> President

e) Trade or occupational information of general interest.

f) Motivational flyers dealing with attitude, problem solving, human behavior, character.

g) Soliciting out-of-town enrollees for interest in housing or employment assistance, or desire to join churches, clubs, or other organizations familiar from home.

h) Sending a birthday card.

Use the phone for:

a) Encouraging parents, wives, husbands, and others to attend orientation.

b) Follow-up of out-of-town enrollees to gain insight into their personal likes and dislikes.

c) Showing concern for personal problems disclosed during the enrollment process.

d) Showing praise and recognition for the quality of letters received, or comments, grades, or accomplishments noted when you contacted references or checked transcripts.

e) Any other sound reason you can think of. But don't be a pest, and by all means don't be phoney.

4. Develop a questionnaire for those who will be housed in dormitories. It is important to match roommates for compatibility. Personal feelings and opinions on smoking, drink-

ing, study habits, night life, music, pre-marital sex, homosexuality, life objectives or religion are important. Send the questionnaire well in advance of starting classes so time is available to match those of similar life styles.

5. Ask graduates or current students who live near the enrollee to establish contact by phone to talk about the school and its placement opportunities.

6. Contact the student counselor at the enrollee's high school to call the enrollee and encourage him.

7. For enrollees from small towns or those who live in metropolitan areas that have their own local newspapers, send an article announcing that John Doe has been accepted at your school. Give supporting material on the enrollee's background and your school.

   In your contacts with the enrollee it is important to remember nicknames (if the enrollee likes it) and names of family members. Write this down so you can refer to it before calling.

These communications will help you to avoid the no-shows and cancellations. Not only is the applicant much more motivated than if left alone from the time of enrollment. He or she is at a psychological disadvantage to cancel as the result of having friends, family, high school counselors and others noting his enrollment and offering praise and recognition.

Chapter 11

Comprehensive Orientation
–A Must!

Many schools compile, sometimes beautifully, a booklet advising their students of all rules, regulations, suggestions and services. We prepared one and we recommend that every school "put it in writing." Words on paper are without a doubt necessary for reference and specific clarification. But by no means should a booklet be a substitute for a comprehensive orientation meeting.

Rarely can we receive an emotional reaction from the printed word that we can from a living experience. A good orientation is a mixture of pep-rally, sermon, parade, show and plan. It's inspection and direction, hope and help and promise. It is selling, selling, selling, selling, selling.

Because your audience has shown up at orientation is no reason to believe they all are confident they have made a wise decision. It is best to assume none has made a definite decision to attend!

With this in mind, draw up an outline that covers everything you would want to know and hear if your son or daughter were anticipating attendance. Make sure that parents, wives, husbands, and anyone else closely involved with the student's objectives are invited to the orientation. If the student's education is subsidized by an employer or agency using counselors, you might consider inviting these people too.

The more people who come to agree with the student's decision to start, the more people will be disappointed by the student if he drops out. Nobody likes to admit he is wrong or that he failed; but it's much easier to excuse yourself than to "eat crow" in front of those who thought sure you'd make it!

As Orientation of new students is so vitally important in your struggle to prevent no-shows and drop-outs, it is suggested that a full day be set aside for this purpose. Saturdays or even Sundays should be considered so that parents and other interested parties can more easily find the time to attend.

Half of the scheduled time should be devoted to introductions, policies, procedures, etc. The other half should be solely devoted to Placement.

Why spend half the time on Placement?

"Getting a good job" is the reason students are coming to your school. As a matter of fact, if it weren't for this desire there would be no reason for your school to exist. How well you attend to this desire is also the factor that will determine your continuing existence.

With this indisputable bit of logic staring us in the face, I continue to be absolutely astounded at how little emphasis is put on Placement and the very complex task of preparing our students for the competitive challenge that constitutes the search for the better job.

I sincerely believe it is still "The most neglected aspect in all of Postsecondary education."

It is this void in our system that has, for many years now, prompted me to devote full time to this subject. I am convinced that thorough "Job Search" training will not only prevent dropouts, but will be the catalyst that will bring your school both security and prosperity.

I am also convinced, however, that to do this effectively, "Job Search" training must be initiated as the student starts his schooling. My views on this are further explained in Chapter 18.

Now, as to the content of your orientation, it is best accomplished by involving all members of your staff and faculty who have a responsibility to the student. This will include just about everybody. The purpose of having many people involved, rather than just one or two, is to have each advise the new students of their job and how they assist students to gain a better education or a better job. Then provide each with the opportunity to make a simple offer: "If I can help you in any way please come and see me."

Having numerous people personally offer to "help at any time" adds strength to the validity of the statement: "we care." Students and guests alike should leave your orientation convinced that accepting the opportunity to attend your school is indeed fortunate.

Have your Head Counselor lead off the program.

His or her major point is motivation. The objective is to convince the students that they have what it takes, and there is no good reason why they can't share the benefits enjoyed by your graduates if they confide in you and never give up. Points to cover might include:

A) Explain the difference between the prevalent high school student attitude and that which you expect at your school. Time is money. No cheating, no playing around, no standing around. Maximum effort is expected.

B) Consider showing a brief motivational film.

C) Explain the value of goals, both long-term and "things to do today." Accentuate the necessity to write everything down.

D) Explain how to be a positive thinker. "If you think you will succeed, you will succeed. If you think you will fail, you will fail."

E) Explain the necessity to analyze and change "your way of life." No more TV addiction, provide for sufficient sleep, provide for sufficient study time, no more association with friends who aren't success-minded, no more social life that interferes with reaching goals.

F) Explain that they should never hesitate to ask for answers or help. "Communicate."

G) Explain that each student assumes the reponsibility of upholding the reputation of the school, and as a result everyone benefits.

Language and appearance should be clean and respectable. It means money in your pocket. Be honest! Anyone seen ripping off the school should be reported in the suggestion box. Stealing doesn't just hurt the school owners, it deprives everyone of services and equipment. When someone robs the school he robs every student. Guarding the reputation of the school is everybody's job and everybody benefits. Employers come to us seeking better people for better jobs.

H) Explain that students will be consulted from time to time. However, no one should hesitate to come up to talk about any problem. They can rely on us to be objective and to guide them with concern.

I) Explain rules and regulations on parking, fighting, alcohol, drugs, destruction of property, reasons for probation, tuition responsibilities, and insurance liability.

J) Explain your attendance policy if you have it. Pass out a written policy if you have it.

The Counselor can then introduce your Chief Instructor or Director of Training who will pursue the following areas:

A) The instructor's credentials.

B) The "must be able to do" lists handed out at the start of each phase of training.

C) Immediate attention if equipment is missing or broken.

D) The grading system.

E) The opportunity students have to anonymously grade their instructors and all other aspects of their schooling.

F) The progress reports students receive.

G) The policy for working on projects after school.

H) Safety precautions, fire-drill procedures.

I) That it is everyone's job to clean up work areas.

J) Explain guarantee of education again; training after graduation, if needed.

K) Offer to help anytime with anything.

The Training Director will then introduce the Placement Director, who details the following points:

A) No other school you could possibly attend will provide you with the "Job Search" training you are about to receive here.

B) It is not our intention to have you simply get a job as the result of your education. Working together, we believe you can get "Your Ideal Job", a better paying position with a better employer. One in which you can advance based on your effort, and most important, one which you will enjoy going to each day.

C) The secrets of how this will be accomplished will be introduced to you at __ pm. (Or whenever you decide to hold your first "Job Search" session.)

The Placement Director will then introduce your Office Manager or Administrative Assistant, who details student services.

A) Student identification card. Good for discounts at local stores.

B) Newscasts, school newspapers.

C) Student records maintained.

D) All goods, books, supplies available. Stress prices if they are below competition.

E) Restaurant. What's available, hours, prices.

F) Posting of honors, other recognition.

G) Prize drawing for students not late or absent.

H) Cash awards to class with best attendance.

I) Special recognition for graduates with 85% average or better.

J) Special awards to graduates with perfect attendance.

K) Student library hours, use.

L) Financial assistance.

M) Assistance with VA problems.

N) Telephone location, use.

O) Special free sessions on a variety of subjects.

P) Make-up work.

Q) Holidays, vacations.

The person giving this segment then details his or her job and offers to help with anything at anytime. He or she then introduces the President, Director, or other official who will complete the program. This talk should be strong and dynamic, ending the orientation with all the fervor and emotion of a coach just before sending the team out of the locker room to complete the biggest game of the season. You might consider these points:

A) You'll be here for a short time. Decide now to do the very best you can. If you have any doubts about putting everything you have into your training, then maybe you're not ready. Don't start. Come into my office after this session and we'll arrange for a refund!

B) For those who will try, they may be assured the school accepts the obligation of training each student to his or her satisfaction.

C) If you ever have a request, a question or a complaint, I will expect you to come to see me. "My door is always open. Don't hesitate!" "Sometimes we can't fulfill every request, but if so we'll explain why we can't."

D) Ask for questions.

E) Wind up the session with a bang:

"I want you to know that we are depending on you to succeed - for your success is our success! If you fail, we fail. We need graduates who will recommend us to others. If we don't have them we will go out of business. We don't intend to let this happen so we are going to push you, encourage you, discipline you, and work you as perhaps you never have experienced, but I'll tell you this. If you've got what it takes to persevere you'll make it. Start with the attitude you won't settle for anything less than the best and you'll make it! Establish a goal now, right now. Visualize yourself walking up to get your diploma - and then getting that job that you want and you'll make it! In short - If you try and never give up, you simply can't fail! Working together, WE simply can't fail."

Chapter 12

Greeting, Impressing, And Communicating With Your New Students

It was a wise man who said: "You never get a second chance to cause a favorable first impression." That's why a comic tries to have the first joke be a big one. After you get a group laughing you can say "applesauce" and draw a favorable response. Die with your first offering and from then on they'll defy you to get them to as much as snicker! During my fling at show business, it was also my experience that when people aren't laughing they have a much greater tendency to go to the restroom. In the school much the same can happen - only your audiences won't return after a recess.

You've spent time and effort making sure you won't have cancellations or no shows - so don't blow it! The two weeks after orientation are touch-and-go. The first days of those two weeks are crucial.

Raise the smile flag. Get out the handshakes, and study faces and names. A warm reception can quiet a lot of butterflies. Because we start classes so routinely, time after time, it's easy to forget how scared, how doubtful, how alone many of these new students are. And although many stand around quietly, each one is questioning whether he belongs. Some are already certain they don't!

Your reaction must be immediate. Get to those who stand alone, who talk to no one. Ninety-nine times out of one hundred they're not anti-social, they're just shy. Encourage them, introduce them to others in the same class who appear similarly withdrawn. Ask a student who has been there a while to talk to the newcomer and assure him that everything will be okay.

Many schools, particularly those with dormitories, use a big-brother or big-sister program. Older students are assigned a newcomer to meet, greet and show around.

Another idea is to form a greeting committee, comprised of students you know to be personable, outgoing and pro-school. Reward their assistance with a nice luncheon. Incidentally these students are also the ones you can count on to form an active alumni association.

John Hauer, president of the National College of Business in the beautiful Black Hills of South Dakota, says you need more than scenery to avoid homesickness. The NCB student senate provides a wide range of activities to help students identify with the college and make new friends. One of the activities is an early-bird picnic in a local park scheduled during the first week of school, which all new students, faculty, and staff attend. Other activities sponsored by the senate are intramural basketball, volleyball, skiing trips, movies, swimming, roller skating, and ice skating.

Acclimating the student to his new social environment is only half the problem. Students must feel they "fit in" academically. Providing the confidence that they can learn is the other half of the new-student challenge.

At Steed College of Johnson City, Tennessee, strong faculty advising serves this end. In addition to fundamental courses in reading, writing and math which assure that no freshman starts "over his head," a course called "Introduction to Learning" is required. Ron Schmelzer, Ph. D., Associate Dean of Academic Affairs, explains that this course does much to prepare and orient each student to handle college courses and concentrate on career development. Integrated reading and study skills are a key.

Student confidence in our instructors is the next obstacle. That first day of class is for many their last day of class. Analysis might show the reason is simply that the student saw nothing in it for him. He was unmotivated, emotionally unmoved, and thus not involved. On that first day the instructor must sell as on no other. Each student must truly belong, be wanted and cared about.

A suggestion is to have all first-day people introduce themselves and name their hometown, high school, hobbies, and what they most want to achieve in life. Have the class applaud after every recitation, it helps to break the ice and encourage the more introverted.

In addition to creating class spirit, this procedure can quickly tell the instructor who the class leaders are, and who most probably will need a great deal of encouragement. A few words of special interest and recognition to these students after class can be all it takes to cement relations.

To find out who are the givers and who are the takers, who know where they are going and who are vague about their destination, you might suggest to Instructors facing a new group that they have their students answer these two questions:

1. If tomorrow you received one million dollars tax free, what would be the first five things you would do with it?

2. If tomorrow you received three wishes for anything not involving money or material possessions, what would you request?

Have students sign their names. You should then have enough material for conversation, motivation, and recognition to last you to the end of the term.

As that first day of class will set the tone for all to come, be sure you remain in complete control. Be friendly but firm.

I attended a Catholic high school run by the Jesuits, a group that obviously maintains a rigid schedule of both physical and mental calisthenics. They all must have attended a course specifically devoted to "the first day of class." Their patterns were all similar. A friendly hello, a casual explanation of the decorum expected, and a prompt physical attack on the first student to get out of line. Some used weapons such as hickory sticks, rulers, or pointers. Some simply their massive hands, pushing down on the head or pulling up with a firm handful of hair. Some were throwers. It was one of these who, almost ceremoniously, chose me to illustrate to other freshmen what happens to those who don't conform. He methodically advanced down the aisle toward me while slowly raising a very wordy Thorndike dictionary over his head.

As I sat in the last row the suspense built and although I was frozen with fear I nevertheless could sense that other faces in the room were smiling with fiendish glee. Ten feet away, nine, eight, seven, the book took flight with the force of a catapult. I closed my eyes. When I opened them Bob Schmina was slumped over the desk in front of me. Hit him right between the eyes. As Father Huttinger then busied himself with those carrying the limp body to the men's room I escaped unharmed. Bad aim or not Huttinger made his point. As I recollect, from then on I was particularly well-behaved. I also recall that for my remaining four years I had a strange kindred affection for Bob Schmina.

Well, you don't need to resort to violence at your school but the old Jesuit philosophy of jumping on the first class-disrupter is pretty sound advice.

With the open chaos that exists in many public high schools today, the products of these environments must be abruptly informed that such nonsense will not be tolerated.

The difference in administering discipline now as opposed to my day is that now you have to explain why!

Very often the kindest word spoken in any language is no. As parents we can understand this. As kids, however, we can't. We are blind to the social, physical, and moral dangers of our requests. We get angered, for to us, no is unreasonable. We react with indifference and slowly close our ears to the logic of authority. We rebel. Likewise as parents our rebuttals to opposition are for the most part emotional outbursts. Often with no more common sense than: "Do it because I say so!" or "This is the way it's going to be and I'm not going to discuss it!"

Further, arguments like: "When I was a kid . . . ," and "You know what my father would have done . . . ," are equally invalid. The fact that your snacks consisted of peanut butter and a crust of bread holds no logic for a child who has been reared in an environment of Twinkies, Pringles, and Ding-Dongs.

If we are going to communicate and maintain the respect of those whom we are trying to direct we must compromise the ideals of our childhood with the mores of today.

Do this and your students will be thankful for the firmness you administer. And considerably fewer students will choose to leave than if discipline is not maintained.

Chapter 13

Your Attendance Policy

The notions we express in this chapter may be termed unreasonable by many, yet we are adamant in believing schools should have a policy which says in effect:

ABSENTEEISM IS NOT TOLERATED!

If you state or infer at your school that X days or hours of absence are allowed, chances are your average student will view them as accrued vacation. Give two days and they'll take two days. Give them ten days, they'll take ten days.

These will be the same folks to first complain about "not learning." There are no rewards in having a liberal attendance policy.

Triangle Tech of Pittsburgh was only one of many to confirm to us the value of a rigid attendance policy: "Our philosophy is based on the premise that poor attendance becomes a habit if the school is liberal about absenteeism. Excessive absenteeism promotes disinterest because the student begins to fall behind his contemporaries, and the end result is eventual voluntary withdrawal or termination by the school."

In addition to initiating what every good school should - the prompt phone contact of each absent student—Triangle Tech designed large signs with bright lively backgrounds and bold black letters. Everyone carried a single word: "ATTENDANCE." These signs were hung throughout the school. Every classroom, hallway, and student gathering area now serves as a constant reminder that school management is concerned about attendance.

Having an unmistakably strict policy on attendance is by no means a cure-all. In fact, it can cause students to drop out - if they don't believe and understand that the regulations were devised with their interest in mind. This of course cannot occur if all we do is present an authoritative demand. Gentle persuasion by use of logical explanation must indicate clearly why and how the student benefits through compliance.

Following is the text of the flyer on attendance that we handed out at Michigan Career Institute's orientation. Such policy must be discussed, and never come as a surprise. Unless, of course, you find some sort of fascination in a mass student insurrection.

WHY ARE WE SO STUBBORN ABOUT ENFORCING THE REGULATIONS CONCERNING ATTENDANCE

At the end of every phase of training, there are students who do not pass simply because of their absenteeism. Many others, although they pass, get grades far below what they feel they should get for the same reason. And every phase we get numerous complaints that "It's just not fair!"

Well, in some instances we can agree that the verified reasons for absenteeism are legitimate and unavoidable. But this doesn't alter the fact that you did miss X hours of training.

Make no mistake by comparing missed hours here to those of high school. About the only similarity is that they contain 60 minutes at both places. At M.C.I. every hour you miss will take dollars out of your pocket. The reason is evident. You either will lose the knowledge of theory or you'll lose the agility which comes with shop work! As most mechanics are paid according to their skill and the time necessary to perform repairs, missed hours of training become evident in the paycheck.

We are not just throwing words around when we promise each student we accept that he or she won't graduate until both the school and student are satisfied that the student is ready to perform in the trade.

Sure, we could toss out diplomas to everyone who showed up now and then through the term of their contract. But we hardly would be performing a service to our student. That diploma would just be so much paper. It would hardly be viewed by an employer as a notable achievement and assure him that the man or woman he was about to hire was of reputable ability.

If you were running this school we think you, too, would come to realize that the needs of the employers who hire your students are of foremost importance. After all, if we don't train students who become accepted by the auto repair industry we're out of business. And we should be!

Over the years we have contacted employers through personal contact, letters, and surveys. We have asked over and over: "What do you want in a mechanic?" The answers seldom vary. First, an honest person; second, a responsible person; and third, people with skills in specific areas.

Why do we stress character and personality traits in our grading system? Simple. That's what employers are willing to pay more to get!

So now you ask, "Well, what does attendance policy have to do with this? I know a lot more than do some other guys in the class, so I can afford to take time off!" We don't think so.

Over the years we have dealt with thousands of employers. When they call to fill a position and we have someone in mind, invariably one question they ask is: "What does his attendance record look like?"

One prominent employer said it all when he remarked: "What good is the best mechanic in the world if he can't show up everyday and be on time!" Get the idea? Every time you are late or absent it is marked down on your permanent record. And every such mark lessens your chance of getting one of the better jobs.

Absenteeism does not just hurt you, however. It hurts your fellow classmates. Every time a student comes to class late he or she interrupts the continuity of the lesson plan. Both the instructor and class are distracted and time is lost.

Absenteeism often results in unnecessary questions by the returning student about the material that was previously covered. The entire class is stalemated for the sake of one student who is attempting to get up to date. Very often this discourtesy is not intentional, but it does, nevertheless, take dollars out of the pockets of every student in class.

For us to determine what absenteeism is legitimate and what isn't would require the full-time efforts of a detective agency. We knew one student with three grandmothers who died. One of them for a second time (he lost track of his lies). We don't intend to play referee: absenteeism for any reason is not excused. And it does affect your grade.

Those legitimately absent can partially offset the time they missed by consulting their instructors and requesting projects which they can perform after class hours.

It is our firm opinion that this policy is in the best interests of all students. It promotes self-discipline and determination that is inherent in any story of success, and it creates the maturity that labels a person: Responsible.

As an accredited institution, we are eligible to participate in federal programs but as such we must conform to many regulations. The Accrediting Commission, The Department of Health, Education and Welfare, and the Veteran's Administration all prescribe obligations concerning placement.

Of these VA is the most exact in its requirements; 50% of students must be placed in the field for which they are trained, with very few exceptions.

Placement, therefore, is a very necessary student service and an obligation we take most seriously.

Even though many students have come in and said, "I'll sign a paper that I don't want placement if I can just be graded on auto mechanics without being graded on courtesy, cooperation, initiative, appearance and attendance," we never could make such a concession. Not only because the school cannot exclude anyone from its composite record, but because we sincerely believe we would not be making a decision in the best interests of the student. We firmly believe that although we make it necessary for many to rephase segments of their training because they have not measured up to requirements concerning attendance and character, we are serving our students to the best of our ability.

We trust you can understand that it is certainly not in the best economic interests of the school to require rephasal at our expense. If there are rewards at all, it is in the letters we receive from graduates, often years after leaving, which say: "Thanks for kicking me in the pants, now I sure understand. I have my own business."

As government with its ambitious politicians seeks to become all things to all people, we need as never before those capable of being masters of their own destiny. Those who can create, build, communicate, and prosper independently. We know that each student we accept has within him or her the power, intelligence, and ability to excel. To be something special. When you realize that only you can make it happen through self-discipline, self-direction and unrelenting persistence, you cannot fail.

Our policies concerning attendance and character will remain steadfast as long as we know they are the catalyst that provides the backbone for achievement. To do otherwise, would be to renege on the personal integrity we have established for ourselves after many years of useless negative thoughts and actions. We see no reason to allow permissiveness that perpetuates failure.

With age comes a certain amount of wisdom. It happens to everyone even though all of us thought we knew the answers years before. In gaining this wisdom failure plays a major role, no doubt about it. To be insistent on making your own failures, however, is not too bright. Learning from the mistakes of others is surely a shortcut to success. We trust you can now better understand our position. If not, then indulge us for no other reason than realizing we have earned the right to determine our own destiny. And our destiny is solely based on your success.

                        Sincerely,

                        Richard N. Diggs
                        President

One thing about attendance policies you must remember: whatever you decide on, enforce! As an accreditation commissioner I often wondered if many schools set policies just because they looked good in the catalog. They sure didn't comply with their own regulations—and guess what? Yes, it took the students about the length of a pipe-dream to figure out the rules were made to be broken.

Chapter 14

Sound Course Objectives

Day after day more books appear that advocate sure-fire formulas of Success. They promise wealth, health, and happiness in various guises—and yet, behind their differences and some fancy words and fancier theories, all of them boil down to a very few indisputable basics: If you want to succeed at anything you must have a goal. And you must be able to visualize yourself having accomplished that goal and be excited about it.

This concept is further discussed in our chapters on Placement and on Counseling Relative to Career Motivation, but to simplify it here, your students will stick with you if they have a plan, know where they are going, and feel they are progressing towards the realization of their objective.

To stand before a class, however, and advocate the personal adoption of such a philosophy will have about as much impact as a surgeon general's warning.

Plans must be understood and must be put on paper. As an educator you must provide this plan. For the course objectives, a broad map with a specific destination. And for subjects, or phases of training, a more descriptive map detailing the crossroads, detours, and points of interest. In short, give to each student a personalized guide indicating the best way to get from one point to another.

At Michigan Career Institute we developed a must-be-able-to-do list for each subject area. These are passed out on the first day of class. Satisfactory completion of each topic or shop project is required. Opportunity for recognition is afforded at each progressive step by requiring the instructor's signature for designation of approval.

The use of these lists provides each student with a specific plan. It encourages him or her to achieve and builds continuous pride. It also serves to eliminate the excuses of those with idle hands.

John Ayre, president of the Flint Institute of Barbering, Michigan, feels that the greatest deterrent to attrition he has discovered is simply to keep students completely occupied. This is sound advice. John says: "I go along with the old saying, busy hands and a busy mind make for happiness." And happy people don't drop out.

Academic subjects don't adapt as easily to progress charts as do subjects with hands-on training, — but the advance notice of specific topics and how they apply to the overall course objective will provide more incentive to do well than if the value of the topic remains vague.

In the first two years of my high school career Latin studies were mandatory. If anyone had given me sound reasons to study this subject—beyond the ability to read some future prescription—I'm sure I would have done better. As it was, having no desire to go into medicine or the priesthood I did only what was necessary to get by. To this day I have discovered little more of the value of Latin unless solving a crossword puzzle can be considered sufficient reward. But I feel no such consternation at the perceived worth of vocational courses. For this reason it seems clear that none of our students should ever be without specific prefaced direction which plainly is of value in the pursuit of his or her chosen career.

Chapter 15

Dynamic Instruction — The Backbone Of Education

No other single factor will cause a mass exodus from your school as will inferior instruction. A class considered to be the dumbest will still be bright enough to recognize they are not being taught. There can be little doubt that after getting the students seated on the first day of class, the greatest priority of any school is providing instruction that satisfies each student.

The enormity of meeting such a challenge is well described in this quote from H. V. Leslie of the RETS school in Baltimore: "The greatest single factor influencing the retention of students is the instructor. He/she must be thoroughly qualified, possess a dynamic personality, great patience, and skill in presenting the subject matter both theoretically and practically - with techniques that reach every student in the class and make each one want to learn. In short, the instructor must be a genius!"

Mr. Leslie's description is accurate. Yet how many responses would come in from a "Genius Wanted" ad for teachers? And of those geniuses who did respond: could they communicate with students? Probably not!

I once had a chemistry teacher who was undoubtably a true genius. But the only thing he was able to get across to the entire class was that he was indeed a genius. He was so brilliant that he was beyond reality. His vocabulary was so advanced we weren't too sure he spoke English. This communications gap led to a frivolous year of self-experiment, highlighted by only two memorable learning experiences: (1) chemicals unwittingly combined can create gases apt to hospitalize whiffers rather promptly, and (2) bubble-gum added to a boiling concoction can cause an explosion able to blow all the windows out of the front of a school.

What we need in our classrooms is more than genius. Not only must instructors know the subjects, they must know how to give them away!

When I was in the school business I was fortunate to be teamed with Al Pribish, our chief instructor. He was knowledgeable in depth, on top of every concept, anxious to help anyone, a master of teaching techniques, and one of the world's biggest hams. Now I have never thought of Al as a genius, although he's quite bright, but really as something more valuable - as a hardworking and unselfish human being.

Those of you who have heard Al Pribish speak, as he has throughout the country, no doubt have sensed the validity of my description. For those who haven't here is a brief version of one of Mr. Pribish's papers on method.

THE MANY FACES OF SHOW AND TELL

Learning occurs in an environment! It was with some surprise that I found the word educate in a dictionary to mean, "To release from within." Listen to that. "To release from within." Many people see it the other way, "to stuff in from without."

CONDITIONED RESPONSES. On some occasions I have witnessed a sort of conditioned response wherein the educator anticipates a "boxed" answer and very frequently gets it. This reminds me of the fellow who has a new puppy in the house and of course it needs to be trained. Even a simpleton knows how to train a puppy to be housebroken, its common knowledge. When the dog messes, you grab it by the scruff of the neck, stuff its nose into the mess and throw it out the door. Repetition seems to be important. Continue every time you find the mess. Jam nose in, throw out the door. The animal will learn to associate, and soon it does. It will mess on the floor, jam its nose into the mess and jump out the door!

READINESS. Obviously to lean purely on a conditioned response has its limits. If I were to name one element as of prime importance in the learning process or the organization of techniques, it would be the principle of readiness. Here in truth is the first law of learning. Methodically we must use our small, precise building blocks towards the development of understanding of some subject matter—and to present information before the student is ready for it only serves to confuse rather than to enlighten. Particularly when there isn't the maturity or background to "handle it."

Picture this situation; a father with his nine-year-old daughter on a train nearing its destination. The dad is a machinery salesman and has a suitcase full of heavy lathe chucks and collets and other assorted parts that make up quite a load. Well, as you might remember, years ago people made a practice of putting suitcases up above on a luggage rack. This little girl in her exhuberance to be helpful and a "grown-up," reaches up to pull the suitcase down over the ledge, and the dad jumps up and says, "Wait a minute honey, you'll pull it over on yourself, you may not be able to handle it." Together they pull the suitcase down. A few years pass and the little girl, now a "teenie bopper." is with a girlfriend and in a particularly giggly mood one day and doing the particularly giggly things that teenie boppers do, and the little girl asks her daddy, "Daddy, what's an affair?" (Tee Hee.) The dad smiles warmly and says, "Oh, it's just when two people like each other for a while and get to know each other." "Oh." (Tee Hee.) More years pass, and the little girl reaches adulthood, marries, and has children of her own. One day she is visiting "Grandpa" and says, "Dad, you're cute. Once when I was a teenager, I asked you what an affair was, I really knew what it was but you gave us a short answer just to satisfy us." Then Dad says, "Honey, I remember. I also remember when you were a little girl and we were riding on a train and you almost pulled a suitcase down on yourself. You couldn't handle the weight of the suitcase and that, my dear, is why I didn't tell you any more about affairs, because I didn't think you could handle it!" This story, although it deals with a moral lesson, shows the wisdom of the dad in selecting the time to teach the lesson or rather not to present it; it demonstrates at least in part the law of readiness.

CONCEPTUALIZATION. Of equal importance is the principle of conceptualization. The mind needs to visualize the forest clearly before examining the trees. Otherwise, the student is hard-pressed to arrive at the reason for the application or the practice of a particular piece of instructional information. The basic idea of what is going to occur must be very clear, almost regardless of the words used to describe it.

I can recall once approaching a junior high school youngster who was busily sanding on a piece of pine. I asked what he was making. He answered he was not sure yet, but I was to check back in a little while! To have an idea of what one is suppose to be learning will serve to eliminate waste or random use of education resources.

TELL 'EM. A concise way to express the application of conceptualizing is:

> Tell 'em what you're gonna tell 'em
> Tell 'em
> Tell 'em what you told 'em

Here we see the learner being directed to visualize the goal first, then direct application, and finally the moment to summarize and re-emphasize the concept.

Here, now, is a usable format for a lesson plan. It can help the instructor organize his thinking so as to formulate a lesson and establish conceptualization of his own:

TOMIPASTA - My Italian friend. Here are the letters of the alphabet that serve to summarize the nine points that need to be covered in a lesson presentation:

T Title
O Objective
M Materials
I Introduction
P Presentation
A Application
S Summary
T Testing
A Assignment

THE TITLE of the lesson is of no consequence other than for reference. However, if advertised or utilized in printed material - the more catchy or clever the dramatization the more it will be remembered. An example is the instructor who dramatizes how resistance and heat are related by cooking a hot dog electrically. The students have anticipated his presentation of the "Electric Hot Dog." However, it is the electrical principle not the hot dog that is important.

THE OBJECTIVE. How many teachers muddle through a lesson and then analyze what they might have accomplished? This harnessing of the horse behind the cart leaves much to be desired, and it says very little for the ability of an educator to know what he is doing. I am happy a doctor doesn't do this; it would be unpleasant to have him operate wondering what he was going to achieve. It is necessary to lay out a plan, to establish an idea of what will occur - in the next hour, day, week or, for that matter, the semester or the course. Some people argue this can be difficult. Of course it is! Equally difficult as it must be for the surgeon or other professional who must deal with variables.

Objectives are usually stated generally: "Work On Engines." These are narrowed down to the specifics. Sometimes there may be primary and secondary objectives. Try to keep the objectives pointed towards what the student and not the teacher will achieve. In all cases the objectives should be clear to the student and certainly to the instructor before the lesson is to begin.

Stating objectives is half the battle. The establishment of a goal or direction is invaluable as it clears both the student's and the teacher's mind and leaves a sense of confidence. It also opens the way for self-learning.

Picture in your own past when you asked for directions and someone cluttered your head with mere specifics like: "Go that way for three blocks to a church which is right across the street from a movie theatre that is on the right hand side. Turn left and go down to the park then turn right by the large oak tree, then go half a mile to the second street light and then. . . . " I can recall the frustration I have often felt because the information coming to me seemed oriented to the person offering it and not to me. I needed a clear route and objectives! The learning process is much the same. Here again, the idea of conceptualization comes in.

MATERIALS. Once the objective is established the list of needed materials can easily be determined. What A/V aids will be used? What additional teaching materials? Which method —is it a lecture, shop time, demonstration? By thinking the lesson through, you can easily visualize what materials you will need and list them, usually in their proper sequence.

INTRODUCTION. The introduction or motivational portion of any lesson is the first they see or hear of the objective and is of prime importance. It's too bad you never get a second opportunity to make a first impression! Some degree of drama; a memorable performance; something to hit them between the eyes to get their attention. Many attention spans are limited. It takes a good performer to keep attention for more than 40 minutes without some re-inforcement device, or a hands-on instrument of one sort or another. Sometimes, depending on the day or time, it will be necessary to re-motivate.

There are many available ways to motivate: money, self-improvement, pride. I remember one new teacher who tried to motivate with fear. He announced to his class: "I figure I can lick anybody here. Any takers?" The captain of the football team stood up. Only the quick wit of the teacher saved him when he said: "Okay, you are on my side. Is there anyone here who can lick us both?"

Creativity is often not recognized or not nurtured. The creative mind can frequently find itself in a hostile environment. I recall once going to a patent attorney and in making small talk, I commented he probably had many college grads come to him with inventions. He surprised me when he said: "Oh, no, college men rarely invent anything." This shocked me. "Why not?" I asked. "I guess it's because they are told all the reasons why it can't be done. If a man doesn't go to college no one told him it couldn't be done, so he goes ahead and does it."

A teacher asked who knew how to divide ten into equal parts. "2½ four times," said one youngster — "Don't be a smart aleck," said the instructor!

Too many of us are guilty of not recognizing creativity or of not nurturing it. How about the "cold turn-off" when the instructor gets one answer to a question? Something is asked like: "Who knows how many pounds of pressure is in an acetylene gas bottle for welding?" and up shoots a vigorous hand at the back of the room. It waves back and forth. "Yes?" says the instructor. "Three or more!" responds the hand waver. "No," the instructor flatly replies and looks elsewhere. "Anybody else?" Don't expect that person to raise his hand again, and don't be surprised if you have a hard time soliciting offerings from any of the class. There has to be a way to tell the student he is wrong without telling him he is wrong. Isn't there a difference between being wrong and not being right?

How many times have I listened over my beer to people beginning a conversation in the local pub. They may be discussing the proper way to claim deductions on a tax form. Remember, the purpose of the discussion was to define tax deductions or exemptions. One man makes a statement. "You're wrong!" says the other. From then on, forget about the purpose of the discussion. Who is right and who is wrong is the new purpose. This happens so many times in a marriage relationship. Many people are professional fault finders, or nay sayers. Unfortunately, so are many instructors.

Harry Truman once said that probably the most difficult job he had was when a young assistant or aide or cabinet member approached him with enthusiasm and vigor with a new idea or at least new to him. To listen, even though he knew it had been tried and wouldn't work. To listen, to not squelch the idea from its inception. I think many of us who teach the same subject over and over can look down on what is an old idea to us, but a revelation to the learner.

PRESENTATION. This is the offering of instructional facts or information. Much of it comes in the text and is often better read than lectured. However, an explanation of principles and their application in a presentation as per an outline will help the student to consolidate the concepts.

Many students are notetakers. Some take their notes almost as a science and unfortunately never deviate. I think this can be both good and bad. But the ability to take notes is directly related to the instructor's ability to present an outline, or organized offering of the material. Any instructor who does not have a practical application he can quickly demonstrate will pass quickly to the wayside.

APPLICATION. Here is the opportunity to prove out the old Chinese proverb:

> I hear, I forget.
> I see, I remember.
> I do, I understand.

Probably the real learning occurs here where the student puts problem-solving ability to the task. John Dewey's philosophy has much to be said for it. I am convinced that learning best occurs by "guided self-discovery." The instructor provides the learning environment, the motivation and pathway and guidance to assure the proper discovery is made. The learner comes upon a principle or usage or accomplishment as a result of his or her own efforts. A further facet of the learning process occurs with the self-evaluation which one has to undertake in trying to teach someone else. In class breaks and bull sessions the learner tries to explain what he thinks he knows. This trying-to-teach-it process often ends in becoming another learning process for the person trying to teach. The debate that occurs between learners is truly a useful and productive learning technique to be nurtured.

A contentment comes with self-fostered understanding. This almost cocky self-confidence is a side effect, it happens as a result of a process. We cannot give someone understanding but we can arrange for it to occur at the time the instructional material is applied.

SUMMARY. This is again to relate the concept. We must reinforce the principles of the lesson and, of course, the application in the student's mind. The student must see the forest clearly in spite of the trees.

The students who are awed by the scope of the lesson might feel more at ease if you present them with the principle of the inverted pyramid. Draw a large inverted V on the chalkboard, then draw a verticle line straight up the center of the V. Explain that as each student climbs up the verticle scale, the width of his/her understanding will expand. This helps take the confusion out of what might appear as a monumental challenge. The student begins to realize that learning is a step by step process. That "the longest journey begins with a single step."

TESTING. To measure educational achievement is another matter. Suffice it to say that a test best serves the instructor and not the student. It is like "taking a student's temperature." It offers an indicator of the work that needs to be done—by the instructor.

Furthermore, we must be careful we don't just teach the test. And I cannot let this matter go without a caution against putting pass or fail weight onto a single exam. The life-or-death type of instrument is much subject to problems. Once-a-week testing is a better approach. The frequency or degree of difficulty of the test is not the issue. More to the point, the instructor and student know where the other stands, so there are few or no surprises at report time.

I've always found it a matter for concern when a student doesn't know where he stands, whether he is passing or failing. And yet I recall a student who always would turn in a test paper with nothing on it. No attempt at all to answer! It took a while before I understood. He was saying: If I put something down, you'll know what I know but also what I don't know. If I don't put anything, you will stand in doubt.

How's this for double talk: once you know what you don't know, you also know what you do know! I believe in frequent test "advisories" for the students.

ASSIGNMENTS. Some instructors seem to want the student to copy the textbook cold: "Read Chapter 8 and answer the questions at the back of the chapter." I'm sure you know how it's assembled. Question 1 is answered in paragraph 1, and so on. This lip-service to education is chilling.

Worse is the paper that is returned to the student without a comment. Just a check mark acknowledging receipt. One instructor had a rubber stamp made that said "acknowledge receipt," and a date. He would stamp each paper as he received it. Soon the student began to submit xerox copies for the rubber stamp. Education — phooey!

Which reminds me of the story of the college professor who was a world renowned expert on Greek history. People came from all over the world to hear his lectures. A new and exciting archeological find had occurred on the Isle of Crete and the professor wanted badly to go to the diggings. Unfortunately, he couldn't because of his commitment to his class. He was lamenting his poor luck when his secretary suggested he cut tapes for the next 16 days of his lectures and go to the diggings. She would each day present his tapes. A great solution! He worked day and night to cut 16 tapes and arranged to have his secretary daily set up the tapes. Away he went to the excavation. As luck would have it, he completed his work there earlier than expected and returned on the 14th day instead of the 16th. He chose to visit his class to see how his students were doing. As he walked down the hall, he heard his own voice coming from the classroom as the tape recorder gave his presentation. And in front of his tape player, 200 tape recorders. No students, just tape recorders!

Assignments too require personality — a purpose! Usually just a few words, an indication that you have the interests of your students at heart, will create the same interest and concern in your students.

And there you have it TOMIPASTA. But this "Italian alphabet backbone" is not all there is to dynamic instruction. . . .

SHOW & TELL. Have you ever seen the youngsters at an early level of school doing "show and tell"? The beauty of this pure presentational situation is worth considering. The expression of absorption - the willingness not only to show but to show off! You can almost hear the spongelike minds taking in the information. For some reason, we leave this pure approach as the outside influences that render the simple show and tell more involved and more difficult.

Discipline rears its ugly head. What are we to say of the issue of permissiveness and lack of discipline? I'm convinced that young people today do crave discipline. They won't "like" it when they get it but they will crave it for the sense of direction it offers. They need to know their limits, the perimeters of can and cannot.—I'm sure, if the Lord had meant us to enjoy permissiveness, He would have issued the Ten Suggestions!

GET IT TOGETHER. The teacher needs to show strength, to always be in control. Young people today have ways of putting things, as when they say someone has "got it together," that to me demonstrate a desire to respect authority and discipline. But the whole issue I speak of here is made up of two parts: student participation, and teaching by example. There is no finer form of show and tell than by example. The dress, the language, the image, the words, the actions, the way problems are dealt with. Believe me: little brother is always watching.

MAKE THEM BELONG. The strength of your recognition, and particularly of peer recognition, is worth much. This recognition can have many forms from simple earned praise, student participation in projects, individual projects, to referral of those who need help. Briefly, whatever makes students feel they belong.

When I tried to categorize the different methods of communicating information while motivating students I realized that a statement is difficult. If we are good at it we tend to "tailor make" a method for each situation and for each individual. This is crucial: the ability of a good professional — whether a doctor, butcher, baker, or teacher — to size up a situation and to deliver the proper method to match the circumstance for the best outcome!

LECTURE. At its best lecture is a lively and dramatic performance that contains evidence not only of understanding of the subject matter but also of its application to the job. A dry and seemingly apathetic instructor will stimulate a dry and apathy. Enthusiasm by the instructor will beget enthusiasm in the students. A special enthusiasm springs from a deep and comprehensive understanding of the subject matter. It is true, today itinerent experts are a dime a dozen; an expert is somebody at least 90 kilometers away from home who carries an attache case. But do you remember mean old Mr. Krauss, who knew high school chemistry in and out, and could recite atomic weights and tables from memory? You knew not to mess with him and yet you admired the man (secretly). An automotive instructor who knows the particular variety of synchronizer assembly for every make and model of a car for the last 20 years is a pretty impressive guy; he commands respect based on his depth of technology. The good instructor will know much more than the textbook.

One of the ways by which he can measure if a lecture is "getting through" is with the use of humor. A story or quip that illustrates a point or a principle is a "Thermometer" of the depth of understanding. If a connotation or pun draws no groan or laughter, he missed the boat!

READING THE SIGNS. You can usually read the signs of the effectiveness of your presentation. The wandering attention, fidgetiness, little or no response to humor, and staring without focus indicates it's futile to continue with whatever method you are using. Change the method. Do a demonstration, pass out some material, take a break, do something, but don't continue on! Remotivate. Otherwise you end up the hypocrite!

Don't expect students to be dedicated and motivated if you aren't. Be sure you don't take your lead from the class "loser." It happens very easily, almost without realizing it. For example, the father who has become intolerant of his son who is just a bit bigger than his sister and likes to pick on her. It seems they are constantly squabbling. Finally, the dad can't take it any more and he says, "Son, you have got to stop hitting your sister, now stop it! Do you hear?" And then what does he do to his son to emphasize his point? You guessed it, he hits him. We often catch ourselves in a dry and lifeless presentation and complain of poor student interest.

When you call on a student to answer a question or a student offers an answer or comment or any other kind of involvement, recognize it! When deserved, offer praise in return.

AHA. Get an "Aha" or brightening of the lecture with a demonstration. The preparation for the demonstration is half the battle. For nothing is so deflating as a demonstration that doesn't come out right. Conversely, nothing beats the excitement of involvement in a demonstration for the first time. The electric moment that you experienced the first time you did it is the same electricity needed by the student. However, for some reason it tends to become less exciting to the instructor through repetition. Not so to the new student! Each one is entitled to that same enthusiasm, that magic moment of "Aha" or "Eureka."

Jimmy Durante tells a memorable story of Ed Sullivan doing a benefit for wounded servicemen at a hospital. He asked if Durante would come and do a small segment. "I can't," said Durante. "On that day I have a contract to do two radio spots." "Oh come on," Ed said, "surely you can find a few minutes and we will rush you back to the radio station." Durante agreed. The day for the show came and Durante went on. He did a seven minute bit. There was applause. Then he did another 40 minutes, right through the radio show. After almost an hour he came offstage to thunderous ovation. Ed Sullivan asked him, why did he stay so long and knew he was in trouble at the radio station. "Look out there and you'll see why." Sullivan peeked out between the curtains and there were two young men — each having lost an arm — applauding like mad with each other's remaining hand!

I don't know whether any of us can generate that kind of love but it sure is a good example. The attention-getters are so necessary: those motivators that we spoke of previously, which make of the demonstrations a learning experience and not just an exposure.

INSTANT AMPHITHEATRE. Often classrooms are not really constructed for a close-up demonstration. At such times I suggest you get the class to help you put together an "instant amphitheatre." Put some chairs on top of tables, arrange the tables in a semi-circle, have some people sit in front of the tables and still others on the chairs that are on the tables. The remainder stand to the side. We find these "instant amphitheatres" help to maintain attention and further demonstrate that you care.

Some demonstrations are best given outside of the classroom. The next time you are fighting a warm spring day take your lecture out to a local park, and sit on the grass. Each year on a warm summer day we drive in the student's cars to the large parking lot of a local public school, then on vacation, where we trace charging system wiring harnesses. The instructor puts miles on his feet running from one group to another and arranging the group to have different experiences on different makes and models of cars. I fully realize not every school teaches automotive. But it's innovative application of your own discipline that will, I'm sure, bring about the same interest from the student.

Vocationally-oriented people have a lot of pride and dignity and to fail to recognize this is an error. To foster and develop it is a much better approach. If you ask for a volunteer from the class, or use the army method of "I need a volunteer, you!" be certain that the volunteer finds success and achievement and not ridicule; or you will have trouble finding another.

ROUND ROBIN. Try a "Round Robin" exam the next time you feel the class is bored. Divide the class into four groups and give the groups ten minutes to devise two examination questions. They can use anything they want: their notes, the textbook. The more difficult the better. After ten minutes have each group read its questions. Now comes the Round Robin. Group #1 (the Arabs) will ask one of their questions, Group #2 (the Finks) will answer the question and Group #3 (the Bananas) will judge the answer. Group #4 (Greeks) will pass judgment as to the value of the question. Here is an interesting scene; Group #1 prepares a question, you give two minutes for another group to prepare an answer and it is your job to select a spokesperson from each group, who is subject to change. A second group offers the answer to the question, a third passes a 1-to-10 judgment (7 is adequate) on the answer, the fourth group passes judgment on the value of the question. Then the originator of the question (Group #1) passes judgment on Group #3 (the Bananas) who are the ones who decided how good the answer was, and finally the fourth group (the Greeks) who passed judgment on the value of the question are judged by the people who answered the original question. Let's pass through that again.

The Arabs (Group #1) ask the question
The Finks (Group #2) answer the question
The Bananas (Group #3) judge the answer
The Greeks (Group #4) judge the question

The Bananas (Group #3) are judged by the Arabs (Group #1)
The Greeks (Group #4) are judged by the Finks (Group #2)

#1 is judged by #4
#2 is judged by #3
#3 is judged by #1
#4 is judged by #2

After much debate and controlled exercises by the instructor the groups rotate. Group #2 asks the question, #3 answers the question, #4 judges the answer, and #1 judges the question.

The Finks (Group #2) ask the question
The Bananas (Group #3) answer the question
The Greeks (Group #4) judge the answer
The Arabs (Group #1) judge the question

#3 is judged by #4
#4 is judged by #1
#1 is judged by #2
#2 is judged by #3

The Round Robin is great for creating total class participation. It encourages each class member to speak up. The class experiences the process of reaching judgments—and, after all, that is what education is all about!

At the end of the period you total the points and the group with the most points receives a free coffee from the group with the least amount of points.

SHOW OF HANDS. The "Show of Hands" is an interesting technique that psychologically makes clear to the class your desire to get total commitment.

When you ask a question and someone offers an answer, ask: "How many agree? I will count hands!" Then ask how many do not agree, once again with a show of hands. Add up the agrees and the disagrees. Then out loud count how many people are in the class total. Requiring every person to make a commitment points out that you are interested in every person there. Some people call this "The Lady or the Tiger."

One of the most inspiring methods I know is to stay after class! Make an announcement such as, "I will be the last one to leave this room every day. If you stay it means you are seeking help. At one time or another everybody needs some help." Also try scheduling regular extra-help sessions. This technique again demonstrates to the class your willingness, your desire to teach.

Competition is healthy in sports, in business and learning, as long as the competitors are fairly matched. When you recognize two or more people who are fairly matched give them a competitive situation. Offer them both the same assignment, a research project. Be sure you reward both.

GOPHER. When organizing students to work together in groups, carefully note which students are the doers, the watchers, and the gophers. It seems there will always be leaders and followers. I really don't think there is anything wrong with having leaders and followers, but it's the "gophers" I am concerned for. When the same individual is time after time the tool chaser, the parts runner, the vehicle of three or four others and continually used by stronger wills, this should be corrected by the instructor.

VISUAL AIDS. Earlier, I had mentioned audio visual aids. I wonder how many have considered mixing class participation with audio visual aids? I believe the best person to run the slide or filmstrip projector is the sleepiest person in class. He will be there to advance the film when you signal him!

How about living training aids? In teaching band and clutch applications in automatic transmissions, we have the students stand and we assign two or three to be the band or clutch. They show on or off by clasping their hands to show upshift or downshift. Each of you in your subject areas can perhaps think of ways to involve students as living audio visual aids. Once again, it is the application of "Show and Tell."

SOME REMINDERS. Never talk to the chalkboards. They listen will but learn little. Never fail to recognize effort. Grades don't always indicate the effort put forth. Find ways to openly reward those who obviously try. William Thompson, director of the Penn Commerical College of Washington, Pennsylvania brought this out aptly: "If teachers would only remember to criticize in private and praise in public, they would not only win the confidence of their students but their respect as well." Never advocate behavior to which you yourself do not strive. Never tolerate less than allowable performance. Take steps to arrange for counseling without delay. Never allow brighter students to belittle those not so fortunate. Charge them with the responsibility of setting an example. Never require a student to read aloud or recite when it is obvious he is not prepared. Never allow boredom. Provide additional interest and challenges.

Remembering well that no list of "Musts-for-Instructors" should be without "Sense of Humor" posted somewhere near the top, we pass along this interesting information sheet used at Northwestern Electronics Institute in Minneapolis. The late Cliff Larson, chairman of the board, local sage, and dear personal friend composed these helpful hints some decades ago. Two to one they'll get the attention of your instructors too!

INFORMATION SHEET: TEACHING TECHNIQUES
TEACHER IS ALWAYS RIGHT???

Any resemblance to omniscience is purely accidental.

KEEP THEM IN THE DARK
Keep the student guessing about how he is getting along. Point out only his mistakes and all his mistakes. Avoid praise lest the student think he is progressing.

BORROW THEIR IDEAS
Do all the thinking yourself. Let your students know they are attending your class to WORK and not to think. If a student gets a good idea, belittle it or tell him you thought of it before-- then use it as your own.

STRESS STUDENT'S INSIGNIFICANCE
Let each student know how unimportant he is. You got along without him once, you can again. Point out how uneducated or untrained he really is—never let him forget it.

TELL HIM OFF
Tell the student what you really think of him. Pick on the little things; tell him while he's burning up—and you're plenty mad yourself. Always give your performance before an audience.

PRAISE THEM (FOR EMERGENCIES ONLY)
Pat the students on the back and praise them whenever there are visitors present. It is well to have the principal or supervisor think "all is well." Do not mind the student's surprise. You can always put them back in their place when the "coast is clear."

Chapter 16

Student—Management Communication

Never mind that you advocate an "Open Door" policy and you stress easy communications at your orientation. Relatively few students will take the time to come in, no matter what their problems.

Much of this can be attributed to the inhibitions of the average student. A gap has existed between the students and the administration at previous schools. The negative attitude grows that "Nobody's gonna be able to help me anyway!" So don't overlook the possibility that you haven't yet convinced your students that you mean what you say.

Plan to hold mass meetings at intervals to reinstill motivation and to repeat the offer of direct communications. Yell loud enough and long enough and sooner or later some start to listen. Most of us will repeat nostrums that our Dad or Mom "always used to say." We remember them because of repetition. If Mom or Dad had only said them once, chances are we would never have dug them out of our memory banks.

Because most students won't come forward to voice their opinions regardless of what we say, we must devise the means to take the pulse of this silent majority. There are several approaches. At Michigan Career Institute a student critique is used at the end of each phase of training. We always found the results invaluable. Each student, assured anonymity, comments on every aspect of the training and actually grades his or her instructor. Being free to express ourselves without fear of reprisal appeals to the most timid of us. Honest, frank and full opinions are the result.

In addition to providing each instructor with the incentive to earn noteworthy grades from the students he or she teaches, these critiques perform another valuable service. They give us the opportunity to respond to problems that otherwise may never surface. And by all means respond. Your students must feel that their opinions do receive your attention and consideration.

Your response can be posted on bulletin boards or gone over orally at a mass meeting. In this answer be sure to give generous recognition to those who offered constructive criticism. This encourages productive thought, rather than acknowledgement of those who are chronic complainers.

The student critique also indirectly allows an opportunity for the student to objectively analyze his own performance. Now, one of the tragedies of our government's anxiety to create "the Great Society" is that we have schooled a generation of people in their "rights" to GET. In so doing, multitudes have grown blind to the need to GIVE. Blind to the fact they will succeed only when they realize they must determine their own destiny.

The mother of one of our former students comes to mind. After putting her son in our care she refused to cut the apron strings. We realized this at the initial interview as her boy remained mute in answer to every question. She responded for him. He was 18 years old but I would have given 100 to 1 odds he never made a decision in his life. He was no dummy, so we accepted him, even though we know our greatest challenge was not teaching him mechanics, but rather to get him to think for himself. The task was much more difficult than we had imagined. I suspect he even called home for approval before going to the men's room. It was further complicated, however, as the mother stopped paying tuition until her boy was graduated and employed.

Now ordinarily we wouldn't give in to such demands as we are explicit about not guaranteeing employment, but we did in this case as the obvious alternative was expulsion and we had far too much empathy for this young man's plight than to simply say goodbye.

We spent hundreds of hours of personal counseling. We even hired him to work maintenance in the afternoon, but his 18-year regimentation was seemingly impenetrable. He could not perform the simplest task without specific direction and one-on-one observation. It was as if he were a robot capable of picking up a broom but thereafter immobile until programmed to sweep. His facial expression was also that of a mechanical man, unchanging. Consequently we were never sure he heard what we said. He seldom responded but when he did it was an unemotional yes or no.

If repetition is the soul of memory, one cliche he'll carry with him forever is: "There are two kinds of people who never get anywhere in this world, those who can't do anything they are told and those who can do nothing but!"

After about eight weeks of exasperation we replaced him on the job. We kept him in school, however, still clinging to the faith we could break his total dependence on others. We graduated him, and placed him on two jobs. He lost both after short periods, holding on only long enough for his employers to realize they were required to fill the role of mother.

Little tuition was ever paid, yet this domineering woman took her case to many agencies alleging we agreed to provide a skill for a price and as that skill did not result in steady employment we were negligent in our offerings. No one took her side, but this did little to convince her son he must escape from dominance and begin to ask himself questions which possibly could lead to the conclusion "I must make it happen!"

The questions on the student critique were designed to do just this. IN EFFECT: "How can the school assist me to succeed," BUT ALSO, "What can I do to help the school do a better job?," AND "How can I change for the better?"

Breaking down the gap between the student body and school management, aside from the policies and procedures that affect everyone, can occur more readily if faculty and staff deal intelligently with individuals. Get to know your students. Show concern. They in turn will reciprocate.

It is particularly valuable that top management be visible and obviously approachable.

My good friend Robbie Robbins, former president of the United Electronics Institute in Tampa, has on numerous occasions advanced the philosophy on this subject that is worth adopting. "I consider the most important responsibility I have as the head of my school is to have each student feel 'I am a personal friend of the President.'" Of course you don't accomplish this objective by closing yourself off in some remote office. You've got to mingle with the troops.

Louis Dimasi, president of Penn Technical Institute in Pittsburgh, also speaks out on the value of keeping in touch. "I personally give several lectures and demonstrations and I periodically assist in labs just to stay close to the students." It's no wonder Lou's school is one of the best!

Taking the pulse of your student body, by any means, is certainly a necessity if your school is ever to be considered exemplary. Another way of accomplishing this is the use of student representatives of classes. Some schools feel this isn't a wise way to go as the class representative often takes on the job as would a union official, obligated to come up with demands simply to prove to those who elected him that he is worthy of his position. Others feel more confident that this format can work to the school's advantage.

At PSI Institute in New York City, President Irwin Mautner says their Active Student Council operates well and has been the catalyst that brought together their faculty, management, and students. If established with forethought and planning it could be worth your consideration.

Some other methods of communication which can be beneficial if done well:

1. Signs through the school detailing hours that counseling and placement are available.

2. Bulletin Boards for specific purposes, that are reviewed and updated at regular intervals.

3. Signs and posters encouraging communication.

Additional methods of influencing individuals who won't come forward to voice their concerns are discussed in Chapter 18. Educate your staff to use the simple psychology presented there. You can enhance student initiative and build a management with its ear always to the ground.

Chapter 17

The Importance Of The Student Counselor

How significant is the procurement of truly effective student counseling for your school? To answer, just add up the amount of student tuitions you would be ahead had your dropouts of last year remained in school. Does the sum stagger you, even a little? Then perhaps it's time that you composed and ran a small classified ad to hire a student counselor.

Many school owners have for years practiced an ad hoc "everyone's a counselor" philosophy, only to decide it doesn't pay. Effective counseling is money in the bank. And the question whether to hire one should not be: Can we afford it? but rather: Can we afford not to!

Charles Davis, director of Parks College in Denver, says: "The biggest thing at Parks that has led to significant reduction of our dropout rates is the concept of qualified counselors. At the present time Parks has two such people. They have divided the student body among themselves. These people were chosen for their counseling backgrounds, and also with the aim to have someone each student can relate to with confidence."

By no means should you hire a counselor just by examining degrees. Anyone who has dealt with sponsoring government agencies should realize this. If your experience is like ours you have already concluded that many of their counselors are badly in need of counseling.

Whomever you decide to hire, do so on a probationary basis if possible. You can't afford to keep a non-productive counselor any more than you can afford a teacher who can't teach.

To measure the effectiveness of a counselor, simply compare the rate of loss for a given period with your known attrition rate for previous periods. Then figure what this means in dollars and cents.

Popularity is by no means an accurate gauge to determine effectiveness. We had one young man whom everybody liked. He was indeed one of those rare people who would do anything for anybody. He strived with all his heart to be everyone's friend. He listened intently to everyone, he was sympathetic to each tale of woe. He was, despite his degree, the poorest counselor we ever had.

Counselors must by their nature be positive optimists who consider problems to be challenges. Keep this in mind next time you are hiring, or considering a member of your present staff for this very important position.

If your school is large enough, you should also keep in mind that a counselor with an ethnic background similar to that of the students he or she is working with can be more effective.

Counseling postsecondary occupational students is somewhat different than that performed in high schools or at two year or four year colleges, if only because the choice of careers has already been made. A casual observer might think this makes the counselor's job simpler. Not necessarily.

Many students, particularly in proprietary schools, have chosen specific job training courses because of their dislike for academics. Proprietary schools are, too, almost the only hope for the nation's high school dropouts. These students realize the necessity for a skilled trade but they approach a return to school with great skepticism. Many from socio-economically deprived environments show up as a result of someone's suggestion and/or because they are subsidized—but they do not yet actually believe they can succeed.

The challenge presented to the vocational counselor is monumental and two-fold. He or she must first make these students believe in themselves, believe they can be somebody and assist them to set personal goals. He or she must then encourage the student to find solutions for all the problems that subsequently may detour them from their destination.

Good counseling is not doing for the students but motivating the students to do for themselves. Whether you hire new or additional counselors or educate current staff members to assume these duties, it is wise to keep that concept in mind.

The following two chapters are devoted to the development of the counselor's skills. However, counselors can by no means provide all the answers. Your own ingenuity must be continuing and constant. No two students are the same. They have unique problems. We must try to provide unique solutions.

Chapter 18

Counseling Relevant To Establishing Career Objectives

Aristotle wrote: "The most fulfilling aspect of man is the sense of competence." Hardly anyone could disagree with this bit of wisdom. But it could be expanded to include: "Or the anticipation of competence."

We can welcome the glory of having reached a noteworthy goal—but our zest for life will quickly fade away if we fail to again challenge ourselves to achieve!

Success is not something we some day acquire. Success is ours that moment when we establish objectives and determine our pursuit will be relentless. It is at this instant we give purpose to our lives.

Without purpose, the most renowned of us will sentence himself to his own dungeon, becoming a partner with despair and darkness. Though living, we are dead.

No man, having a goal and believing he could reach it, ever committed suicide, or ever will, unless that goal is death itself. Only when we assess our present as meaningless and lament the losses of the past with no optimistic view of what still can be, do we concentrate on self-destruction.

It is, therefore, significant to all of us that we provide anticipation in our lives. The more plans we have, dreams we dream, goals we set, toward which we progress with the realization of fulfillment, the happier our lives become.

Unfortunately most of us live in dependency on minor but anticipated pleasures such as a TV show, a card game, the Saturday night dance, the hunting trip, the boat cruise, Christmas, a birthday. I use the word unfortunately because too many of us don't establish long-term challenges of major significance that can create lasting enthusiasm.

A steady progression toward long-term objectives can keep us at a relatively steady "high."

Relying only on short-term objectives can play havoc with our emotions. Those who get involved and become busy working on a project know what it is to have completed the project without having set additional goals. It's a definite "low."

Going back to my high school days, how well I remember the agony of doing nothing. They called it the "Jug Room." Those who were guilty of breaking, or even bending, school regulations were sent there. Although always accused unjustly or with mitigating circumstances I nevertheless was sentenced with frequency. At the sound of a bell, a husky Jesuit would proceed to the front of the room and mark a small circle on the chalkboard about the size of a silver dollar. You then sat erect and stared at the circle for the duration of your sentence. If you moved your head, time was added. If you chanced to look out the window or slumped in sleep, you found out very promptly why the Jug Room Jesuit was always husky!

The weakest mind among us would conclude as I did: "Hell is having nothing to do!"

Fortunately the school embarked on a new building project and, being underfinanced, chose to use the "Jug boys" to perform physical labor. It was a welcome reprieve. Having built a considerable portion of the gymnasium, which was ready for use about the time I graduated, I still have some resentment that a plaque was not mounted in the foyer in commemoration of my efforts.

Effective counseling is assisting students to have things to look forward to. This chapter deals with longterm goals: "Establishing Career Objectives."

Following is possibly the shortest course on "Career Counseling" you'll ever find, but one that has worked for us. Conscientiously applied we believe it will work for you!

1. UNDERSTAND that "There is only one way to get anyone to do anything, and that is by making the other person want to do it!"

2. UNDERSTAND that there are but four reasons anyone does anything, and these are:

   a. RECOGNITION. The thought of being respected, set apart from others, being the best, receiving praise, gaining applause.

   b. ROMANCE. The fun of an avocation, adventure, excitement, travel, exploring the unknown, sex, emotional highs.

   c. MONEY—and what it will buy! Food, homes, cars, boats, retirement.

   d. SELF PRESERVATION. Escape from death or injury, good health, long life.

3. REALIZE that because these are the sole reasons anyone does anything, they are also the four great motivating factors of mankind. They are the only tools you need to motivate if they are presented intelligently to those among whom you have gained respect.

4. You can best gain the respect of the student you are trying to inspire through inviting him to talk to you and by break-

ing his preoccupation with use of the four great motivating factors. For example:

a. Using RECOGNITION: Tom, I hear so many stories about all this potential you have, that I'm really curious about your future. How about meeting me at noon today to discuss some ideas?

b. Using ROMANCE: Tom, someone told me you like to race cars. I'd like to talk to you about that. Maybe someday you'll be in the "Indy 500." How about meeting me at noon?

c. Using MONEY: Tom, I'd like to talk to you about using your talents to make a small fortune. How about meeting me at noon today?

d. Using SELF PRESERVATION (not always applicable to the situation): Tom, I've got a few sound ideas on how you can get out of the ghetto before you get killed. Meet me today and I'll lay them on you!

Often you can combine two or more of these motivating factors. In any case you are making the student want to meet you, and when he or she keeps the appointment there will be a predisposition to hear and accept what you have to say. Isn't this better than sending a note that requires the student's presence in your office? Sure, that student will show up - but full of doubt, resentment, and fear. Hardly the right climate for a productive counseling session! The student must talk freely and openly. If you can't both communicate then you can't counsel. When the decision comes to make a fundamental change it must come from the student. No counselor can simply lay out a blueprint for another person and expect it to be adapted and pursued.

5. That first counseling session sets the tone for all sessions to follow. It is essential that you get the student to like, respect, and trust you. You can do this by using the following foolproof formula.

a. NEVER ARGUE, NAG, HASSLE, OR CRITICIZE.
b. OFFER PRAISE, RECOGNITION, AND HOPE.
c. MOTIVATE SOME DEFINITE ACTION.

This formula, of course, works well with anyone, not just students. As a counselor in training you might try it out at home tonight. There is certainly no better laboratory for experimentation than within your primary environment. Make a commitment on paper before you leave your office.

I will not criticize my wife, my kids, my parents.
I will not argue.
I will not nag.
I will not hassle.
I will compliment.
I will praise.
I will offer hope by encouraging others.
I will make others want to do things by offering incentives that coincide with their motivating factors.

Incidentally, you'll do better at handling people if you recognize what is the primary motivating factor of the individual you are trying to influence. Everyone is susceptible to being influenced by all four: recognition, romance, money, and self preservation; but we are turned on in varying degrees by each of these factors.

Only after you have succeeded in utilizing this formula as a way of life can you expect to be an extraordinary counselor. Read your written commitment constantly, day in and day out, until your actions in dealing with people become second nature.

Being impulsive as I am, every now and then I'll "blow my cool" and openly criticize a member of my family or an employee. This generally occurs because it is still necessary to maintain firm control with discipline whether you are dealing with kids or employees—and, of course, this opens the door for excuses, rebuttal and argument. Should it occur to you, don't forsake the communication you are trying to develop by being stubborn and egotistical. Apologize—and do it promptly.

6. Now we come to the "nitty gritty" of motivating students. Assume you have succeeded in getting the student to your office and it is apparent he or she is comfortable in your presence and not hesitant to talk. You may proceed. But if the student is still not smiling, not responding with lengthier answers than yes or no, nor apparently at ease, you are not ready to proceed. Spend some more time breaking down the barriers. It may take a long while with some students but be patient, and be positive. Do not tell the student how bad he is.

In addition to the fundamental methods of handling people we have already discussed, use these helpful tools:

a) SMILE.
b) ALWAYS ADDRESS THE STUDENT BY HIS NAME, OR HIS NICKNAME IF YOU KNOW HE PREFERS IT.
c) BECOME GENUINELY INTERESTED IN OTHER PEOPLE.
d) BE A GOOD LISTENER.
e) TALK IN TERMS OF THE OTHER PERSON'S INTERESTS.
f) USE HUMOR AND PERSONALITY.
g) MAKE THE OTHER PERSON FEEL IMPORTANT.

If you are wise enough to use these suggestions with persistence, sooner or later that student will arrive at the state of mind where he or she must decide to dramatically change an earlier way of life, for the sake of a better way of life.

(Note: In the rest of this explanation I shall refer to the student as him rather than him or her. Not that I'm a chauvinist, but for the sake of easier writing and reading it makes sense to use this convention.)

Now, when you are satisfied you have gained the respect and friendship of the student it is time to introduce the fundamentals of a "fool-proof success formula." You must decide at this point whether you want to lay out the whole system at once or take it a session at a time. If you're dealing with a youngster who has never accomplished anything in life you are better off taking it day by day.

SESSION ONE:

Introduce the student to the three fundamentals of handling people (above), after impressing him with the idea that if he is ever to succeed at anything it will be because he makes it happen. He alone will determine his destiny. The student must realize he has the power to control the positive and negative influences of his life; he has only to become the dominant factor. Assignment (provide in written form):

1. Every time you think or say a negative thought stop when it dawns on you and perform some action which is unaccustomed, such as calisthenics, or jotting down a mark on a scorecard you are carrying.

2. Carry a pocket reminder which reads: "I am the master of my life. It is within my power to have what I want and to change whatever can be changed." Repeat this no less than one hundred times a day. Say it out loud when possible.

3. Come to see me tomorrow at AM/PM.

SESSION TWO:

Record all the positive things that occurred as a result of the assignment given in Session 1. Praise the student for his efforts. Then make the student aware that he will only achieve outstanding success if he:

a) Establishes a specific GOAL on paper which is both something he would like to do and realistic.

b) Establishes a specific DATE at which time the goal is to be reached.

c) Keeps a list of all ITEMS that must be accomplished before obtaining the goal can become fact. He must review this list daily.

d) Establishes, from the above list, a "Things I will DO TODAY" list on paper. Carries this with him. Crosses out items as they are accomplished. Reviews this list every night. Establishes a new list every morning.

e) PERSISTS. Never allows himself to think he can't. Gains the attitude that giving up cannot be tolerated.
Ask the student at this point if he is prepared to pay the price of greatness. If he responds enthusiastically, offer to assist him to make dreams come true. If the student says no, or he is not sure, simply tell him that you'll be happy to help him when he feels he is ready. For those who want to proceed, assign the next project. Assignment:

1. Sit down tonight and write out everything you like to do. Then list each item numerically with a rating system from one (1) to five (5), with 1 indicating it is among your most favorite things to do. This list should include jobs, hobbies, sports, education subjects, and so forth.

2. Continue the assignments given in the first session.

3. Come see me again at _____ AM/PM on _____.

SESSION THREE:

Ask if the student is feeling the effects of people reacting favorably to him as the result of the manner in which he is now handling people. Record all the positive things that occurred as a result of continuing to use the formulas provided in the first session.

Ask if he feels more confident as a result of continually telling himself that he is the master of his own destiny.

Utilizing the list the student has prepared of items he likes, ask if he came to a conclusion as to what he would most like to do with his life. If the answer is yes, and it should be, your job has quickly become easier. You can proceed to another assignment. If the answer is no, then proceed to ask questions about careers that coincide with the likes of the student. By no means should you make a decision for the student. When a conclusion is drawn, it must be the student who draws it. And again the goal must be realistic. One in which the student can visualize himself actually accomplishing the goal.

The most accurate description of happiness I have ever come across is simply this: "Happiness is the progressive realization of a worthy goal with the thought of being able to achieve it!"

ADDITIONAL SESSIONS should then be held at the intervals you determine to be necessary to eliminate old habits and create a new way of life—a positive way of life.

Keep in mind that for any person to retain enthusiasm, the fire of desire must be fed. Many good books are available dealing with success and happiness. Get your student into the reading habit by giving, recommending, or loaning books—but with the understanding they must read for a specific amount of time each day. If possible, at a preset hour of the day.

Generally, you can tell that your counseling has been successful when students look you up to report their progress. They will possess an unmistakable enthusiasm for life, and are anxious to share results of their new-found philosophy.

The suggested procedures you have just read are to use with individual students. This is very time consuming, of course, so it well could be that it is impossible for one person to get to all those who could use some help.

This may not be a problem, however, if your school adopts the "Job Search" training program advocated in the next chapter on Placement. This policy stresses the significance of holding your first "Job Search" training session on the same day as orientation. And the first order of business in that session is showing students how to focus on specific employment objectives that are individually desirable.

Chapter 19

The Science Of Placement . . . .

Perhaps The Most Misunderstood And Neglected Function On U.S. Campuses, Yet The Single-Most Important Factor In Controlling Attrition

Over twenty years ago, I set up my first Placement Department, never realizing that someday it would become my life's work. I hired a woman experienced in Employment Agency work and said: "Just get on the phone and keep calling employers." "We've got to line up jobs for our graduates."

I felt an obligation to place these kids even though we made it clear that "We don't guarantee placement." After all, what good is any Career education if it doesn't lead to a paycheck?

So that was about the extent of our placement service. Sure, we spent a few minutes telling each one to smile, speak up, dress appropriately, and be on time, but seldom much more than that. Then we handed out slips with the employer's name on them and said "Good Luck."

It took many years before it dawned on me that this type of Placement Service was a mistake. And in the interim, I repeated this weakly-thought-out concept over and over again. At the Business Schools and Colleges, with which I have been associated, we added some time for Resume preparation and how to respond to interview questions but basically the procedure was the same.

Sure, the majority of my kids got jobs, but many at meager wages, many with unscrupulous employers who out and out lied about earnings, many with those who withheld wages and then closed down, many with those who wanted more than just an employer-employee relationship, many with those who only paid lip service to giving a damn about the employee, etc., etc., etc.

Chances are that over the years the average placement at all my schools didn't last six months. In retrospect, I have to admit I never gave this much thought. But one thing for sure, I was much more concerned with my placement statistics than I was with the types of jobs my graduates were getting. And I have to smile as I think back to my early years. We didn't provide Placement assistance, we were simply a referral service. As a school, we should have taught our students "The Science of Getting and Keeping Their Ideal Job."

I can remember being irritated with students who turned down any job for which we furnished the lead. I didn't want to listen to the student's reason for saying no. I truly was blind!

Without boring you with all the details of why I proceeded to explore every facet of this little known science, I can say that I am no longer blind. After thousands of interviews and years of research, I see as few others and as a result I am frustrated as few others. The "Job Search" training that we provide for our graduates throughout all of Postsecondary education is deplorable. Although I must admit that proprietary occupational schools are much more conscientious than those in our 2 year and 4 year colleges.

The truth is, however, that in most all schools, we don't consider the most important aspect of human endeavor; to be happily employed.

I can't tell you how many times I have seen this scenario replayed: A student, lacking self confidence, says "yes" to the first job offer received. He or she is ecstatic, but within a week or two quits for one of a thousand reasons and comes back to say, "find me something else."

We then offer sympathy for the "traumatic experience" he or she has had and promptly repeat the same pattern, ignoring the obvious; teaching the student how to research prospective employers.

You have certainly heard the old adage, "Give a man a fish and you feed him for a day, . . . teach a man to fish and you feed him for a lifetime." Well, I can't think of a lesson that more aptly applies to this business of placement, and yet at all levels of Postsecondary education we continue to function in the same antiquated manner: We provide leads and little more, . . . thus creating dependence on the school. In contrast, isn't it apparent that if we taught students the skills necessary to find and obtain their own jobs that we would be providing them with self-reliance that would last a lifetime?

The "Science of Getting a Job" is a very complex subject today. Due to advancements in hiring techniques, it is considerably different than it was just ten years ago. Ideally, an applicant for a better position should have an understanding of Psychology, Advertising, Marketing, Human Behavior, Public Relations, Salesmanship, Organizational Planning, and Time Management. And in addition be ready to show off an exciting personality, while maintaining self-discipline and a stubborn resolve to persist.

Everybody in the field of Placement would probably concur with this assessment. They would probably agree, too, that thorough "Job Search" training is needed more than ever before, and that few students, if any at all, have even a remote idea what they are up against. And yet, to our knowledge, there is not one college in this country that has a credit course on this subject that is required to graduate in any discipline. Further, only a handful of occupational schools hold "Job Search" classes in which attendance is mandated and a passing grade is a must.

Is it any wonder why so many of our graduates fall short of their expectations?

To contend, as many do, that our graduates should possess the desire, motivation, and maturity to research this subject on their own is a ridiculous assumption. Practically everyone thinks they know what's involved in getting a job. It is only after experiencing the pain, frustration, and despair associated with rejection, and often making the wrong decision, that wisdom is expressed.

And don't think for a moment that it is only those with lesser grades that have problems associated with placement. We recently talked to a graduate in Electrical Engineering who graduated number one in his class. He had numerous well paying offers, and proceeded to take one which required relocating his wife and family about 1000 miles away. He quickly found out that while the money was good, management was hostile, the hours expected of him were beyond reason, and the stress of the job was leading him straight to divorce court. Brilliant as he was, he never considered how significant it was to perform research on all prospective employers.

This story is not an isolated incident. Mistakes like this occur thousands of times daily at all levels of employment.

In recent years, numerous studies have been made of the American employee. The results have varied little. All have shown that between 70% and 80% of all U.S. workers are not happy with their jobs.

Another study which appeared in Forbes magazine revealed that the average U.S. employee works at a pace equal to 30% of his or her productive capability.

Now knowing with certainty that those who enjoy their jobs are considerably more productive, can you imagine what our economy could be if we reversed the happy-with-their-job statistic so that 80% of our workers were satisfied? Chances are we could at least raise the productive pace of the average worker to 60% of ability, and consequently double what we are producing today.

Is it reasonable to believe that we can teach people how to be happy with the jobs they now have? I don't think so.

Is it reasonable to believe that we can teach people how they can find a job that they will unquestionably be happy with? I definitely believe so!

All we have to do is require comprehensive "Job Search" training as a prerequisite to graduation from all postsecondary schools.

Is this realistic? Certainly not in the foreseeable future, but in time, yes! Those schools who are conscientiously teaching this subject will reap the harvest of benefits, and this will encourage other schools to get in line.

HERE ARE JUST A FEW ADVANTAGES THAT YOU WILL NOTICE ONCE THIS TRAINING IS STARTED:

* Your students will become more self-reliant. They will understand that their success in life will come to them as the sole result of their own actions. The entire attitude of your student body will be healthier, . . . more mature. Few will thereafter contend that "It's the School's responsibility to get me a job."

* As the result of students gaining the knowledge and confidence to seek positions with employers of their choice, you will see a marked increase in the average starting wage gained by your graduates.

* As the earnings of your graduates increase, your default rate will decrease.

* As the result of the placement achievements of your graduates, the image of your school will be enhanced. And in the school business, reputation is security. Nothing you can do will steadily bring referrals in the door as will a consistent chain of superior placements.

* Students focused on very specific personal employment objectives will not drop out.

If what we have covered so far in this Chapter makes sense to you then please read the following suggestions carefully. Almost certainly they are considerably different than the procedures you now use.

TO HAVE "JOB SEARCH" TRAINING THAT WILL KEEP STUDENTS IN SCHOOL . . .

1. Hold your first class the same day as your orientation.

2. At this first session:
   a) Provide a comprehensive text for each student which covers goal setting.
   b) Show each student how to choose the specific employment objective that is "just ideal."
   c) Introduce the idea of "Job Groups" making sure that every student belongs. These groups of 3 to 5 students will meet periodically to share employer research, offer personal suggestions and ideas, practice role-playing of telephone and interviewing techniques, and be a nucleus of mutual support.

3. Provide general meetings scheduled throughout the year at which attendance is mandatory and passing grades are a prerequisite to graduation. The purpose of these sessions is primarily to keep the eyes of all students focused on their employment objectives. Topics of importance should include information that will . . .

   a) Show students how to locate those employers who are the best to work for and who could be in a position to offer the "Ideal Job."
   b) Teach students how to go about researching all prospective employers.
   c) Provide suggestions on developing V.I.P. contacts who can help students get their "Ideal Job."
   d) Introduce the idea that employer research must precede the development of a resume.
   e) Cover the variety of resumes that might be used and why.
   f) Provide information on what employers want to hear today.

    g) Provide tips on preparing for a job interview.
    h) Provide tips on how to act during an interview and how to close the interview so that the candidate can "stand out" from the competition.
    i) Provide tips on how to follow-up after the interview.
    j) Provide tips on how to advance in pay and position after being hired.

As you probably realize we humans are all very happy when progressing nicely towards goals we have set for ourselves. That's why it is so important that your Placement activity coincide with the start of school rather than at the end.

Education is merely a tool that helps a person achieve his or her employment objectives. At all levels of postsecondary education we often lose sight of this point. We don't understand why students aren't motivated. The reason is obvious: They have no idea how they can use their education to make a living. For them the future is too obscure, too vague. They have doubts as to whether they are on the right road. It is this uncertainty which often leads to dropping out.

Education itself is not the goal of our students. They come to us for jobs. It is time we realize this and put the emphasis where it belongs, on employment objectives, not educational objectives.

If from the day students start your school, you assist then to create plans with very specific employment destinations, you will eliminate the possibility that doubt and confusion will cause another student to prematurely say good-bye.

OTHER SUGGESTIONS RELEVANT TO PLACEMENT THAT ARE WORTH CONSIDERING

1. If you can possibly arrange it, have all your current students attend each graduation. Then as each graduate comes forward to receive his or her diploma, the commentator can acknowledge those who have already accepted an offer of employment, the name of the employer and the starting wage. This procedure enforces the desire of those still in school and motivates them to work harder.

2. Print all placements in your school newspaper.

3. Anytime you receive a letter from a graduate, telling of his or her accomplishments, make numerous copies. Put them on bulletin boards and in the reception area where applicants wait. Your reps might also send copies to enrollees who have some time to go before starting school. They will help to prevent no-shows.

4. Invite personnel managers, Corporate V.I.P.'s, successful graduates to speak at Graduations and other student assemblies. Ask them to detail their experiences in hiring and being hired.

5. Contact employers where your graduates are working. Ask them for their suggestions as to how you might better prepare students for the jobs they offer.

6. Survey your graduates. Ask them for their opinions as to subjects which should be added to the curriculum and those items which should be covered more thoroughly. Also find out if they are pleased with their jobs, and if not, why not.

7. If you assist students to get part-time jobs while they are attending school, make sure these jobs are related to the students' career objectives if at all possible. A graduated list of relevant experience is important when preparing a resume. Many employers and Personnel Managers consider this factor to be significant.

8. If you provide a service for employers by referring students for part-time jobs, make sure the employers agree to your terms.
   a) The hours worked should not interfere with school hours or deprive the students time to get sufficient sleep.
   b) No offers of full-time employment should be made which would prevent the student from completing his training.

9. When one of your graduates accepts or is promoted to a very impressive position, take the time to write a public relations release. Send it to all local papers, particularly in the area where the graduate resides.

SUMMARY

Placement is the key to the continuing success of your school. It makes higher education,—hire education. Do it well, as few others, and you will forever be sought by applicants and envied by your peers. And your reputation will endure.

Editors Note:

If you would care to review several books written by Richard Diggs for "Job Search" training as outlined in this chapter, write or call:

Progressive Publications
P.O. Box 4016
Homosassa, Florida 32647
(904) 382-1452

Chapter 20

Counseling Relevant To Problem Solving

Too many people have advised me that students are always going to have problems and they will drop out because of them. "And that's life!" I don't believe it. Not that we can solve all ills, but we can certainly be instrumental in helping to solve many.

Problems will remain problems only when we do nothing to change them. Despair sets in when indecision becomes our constant companion. The greatest problem-solving technique known to man, therefore, is "make a decision!"

If it's wrong, make another one. If that's wrong make another one. If that's wrong make another one, and so on and so on. Do this with persistence and forethought and no problem will continue to puzzle and obstruct.

Effective counseling relative to problem-solving, therefore, is simply to assist students to make decisions.

The formulas introduced in the previous chapter should allow you to win the ear of the student, once you become aware that a problem exists. Unfortunately, in many instances, the student is gone before the problem has been brought to the attention of a counselor.

Every member of your staff must become aware of negative changes in behavior and personality and refer the names to counselors promptly. If periodic counseling of all students is a standard practice at your school, the student may not feel he is being singled out for attention when asked to meet with the counselor.

At this time it is important to ask questions—questions that don't require a yes or no answer. Then be a good listener. Often it is great therapy for the student just to have someone to tell his troubles to.

After listening to his story, if you feel the student is definitely mistaken in his thought process and he rather than others is responsible for his problem, you confront the most difficult phase of your counseling process. You may well feel like prefacing your response with: "Well, you damn dummy!" But you must stay in control. If you expect to change the student you can't afford to arouse resentment. Consider using the following suggestions:

1. Begin with praise for whatever you find in his story that is worthy of recognition.

2. Call attention to his mistakes by telling of your own mistakes, or of others you have heard about. Tales about the goofs of prominent people who gained respect can be significant.

3. Ask questions, rather than giving direct orders or concluding you have the answer.

4. Never embarrass or cause a student to lose face. So many of us seemingly take pleasure in proving another person wrong, then gloating about it. You may win an argument but you'll lose a student!

5. Despite your immediate feelings to the contrary, try as honestly as you can to see things from the student's point of view. Place yourself in his environment.

6. Express interest in the student's ideas and desires.

7. Give the student a fine reputation to live up to. Appeal to noble motives.

8. Dramatize your ideas and suggestions but when the student seems to respond to one of them let the student feel the idea is his or hers. Offer praise to the student for his or her "good thinking."

9. Throw down a challenge. A statement to the effect: "Boy!, if you are able to do this you are really a magician!" or some similar acknowledgement that builds confidence and enthusiasm can work wonders!

10. Set a time for the student to get back to you with the results of his efforts. Having someone to brag to is important. I personally dread the thought of getting a hole-in-one while playing golf alone!

As comprehensive as these suggestions might appear there will be many times when the solutions are elusive. Don't feel you are wasting your time!

When faced with what appears to be a monumental problem, far too many students will impulsively decide to quit. "Buying time" with the student can result in a much more mature decision.

You may wish to develop—or even to contract—counselors who are proficient in specific areas, depending on the size of your school. Western Business College of Portland, Oregon found success in problem-solving when a retired University professor was hired to work three days a week. He talks with every student in school and, as more or less an outsider, he is viewed as an impartial observer when presented with school-related problems. "If he feels he has not saved a student, he informs the student's enrollment officer who in turn tries to find solutions." This is wise advice. If we as counselors aren't "hitting it off" with a student, don't beat a dead horse. Get another member of your staff to pick up the ball.

The Knapp College of Business of Tacoma, Washington covers various alternatives in counseling by having a variety of members on a Retention Committee. Throughout training the committee surveys the student's opinions. Problems divulged which the committee cannot handle are referred to a qualified guidance counselor.

If you don't have the need for a fulltime counselor or you lack counselors capable of handling complex psychological problems, you might consider the approach of United Electronics Institute of Tampa. "We have a professional counseling center under contract to work with our students. It offers both a psychiatrist and a psychologist. This service has not only proved helpful in student retention, it has given us some heartwarming experiences. One young woman in our program was on the verge of divorce; as a result of the service, the marriage was saved and the student is graduating."

A man whose practical contribution to occupational education equals any made in this country is M.Michael Freedland, now President of the Philadelphia Offset Printing School. Mike's concern for his students is an example to all of us. Together with his able assistant Jack Rosenfeld, Mike has compiled for his inner city student body a complete list of problems and the possible remedies that is indicative of sincere forethought. This school is prepared for problems and as a consequence its calm reactions and sound advice avoid further alarming the student. The school's confidence that a solution can be found is really contagious.

Years ago, as an accrediting team member, I had the pleasure of visiting Cleveland's Westside Institute of Technology. Rarely in a lifetime do we meet people as generous as Westside's president Dick Pountney. His commitment to problem-solving went beyond my comprehesion, and it sure wasn't restricted to 9 to 5. At any hour, on any day and at whatever expense of effort, Dick was available and alert. One particular case sticks in my mind: a student of ability who was losing the battle with the bottle, a classic alcoholic unable by himself to withstand temptation. Most of us, faced with this situation, might say goodbye. Pountney arranged and paid for the student to live and dry out in a sanitarium. The cost? More than the man's total tuition. But the student stayed on the wagon and he did return to graduate and get a good job.

Pountney chose to make other such investments. A nice guy but a dumb businessman? Maybe. But his school enrollment has more than doubled since my visit. Moreover, few schools receive editorial praise such as comes unsolicited to Westside Institute. Now you may not care to commit the time or resources that Mr. Pountney personally places at the disposal of his students—but you should know the exact available channels for treating various personal problems. Chances are that your community has a complete guide to community services. Get copies. If no listing exists write your own. Many of the solutions you can recommend cost little or nothing. Provide the agency names, addresses, and phone numbers. It's easy to say to a kid, "Why don't you see somebody about that problem?" It's another matter to refer him or her to a specific service! Consider what resources you might recommend for:

1. Abused children (sources of protection)
2. Aged Living Accomodations (for parents or grandparents)
3. Alcoholism (best sources of treatment)
4. Allergies (may occur as result of products used in your training)
5. Ambulance (closest to school)
6. Arthritus & Rheumatism (best sources for treatment)
7. Burns (best sources for treatment)
8. Cancer Detection (best sources for analysis)
9. Chaplain Services (all denominations)
10. Child Guidance Clinics (best sources for testing physical and emotional behavior)
11. Civil Rights (best sources of information)
12. Clinics (sources of free care)
13. Community Centers and Settlements (often good sources for ethnic housing and social life)
14. Counseling—Adult, Family, Marriage (best sources of free or low-cost professional assistance)

15. Convicts Aide—(best sources for assistance and rehabilitation)
16. Courts (knowing and communicating with judges can pay dividends)
17. Credit Unions (those with open membership which can provide credit not available at banks)
18. Cultural Activities (helpful for out-of-town students with particular interests)
19. Day Care Centers (in various locations)
20. Deaf and Hard of Hearing
21. Dental Services (free of low-cost treatment)
22. Diabetes (diagnosis and treatment)
23. Divorce (free or low-cost legal assistance)
24. Drugs (best sources of treatment)
25. Epilepsy
26. Eye Banks, Clinics
27. Family Planning
28. Financial Assistance—Debt consolidation (best sources of free or low-cost assistance)
29. Food Stamps (where and how to apply)
30. Foreign Born Services (where your I-20 students can get assistance)
31. Foster Children (best sources of information)
32. Genetic Counseling (best sources of information)
33. Government Benefits (know addresses and phone numbers)
34. Halfway Houses (helpful for providing a better environment for certain students)
35. Homeowners & Mortgage Counselors (sources of free or low-cost assistance)
36. Hot Lines and Rap Lines
37. Housing Services
38. Immunization Clinics (free or low-cost shots)
39. Labor Relations (assistance with job-related problems)
40. Landlord-Tenant Problems
41. Legal Aid (free or low-cost assistance)

42. Maternity Services (free or low-cost assistance)
43. Mental Health
44. Missing Persons
45. Nurtition
46. Poison Control & Information (phone numbers for quick reference)
47. Pregnancy (free or low-cost detection, advice, treatment)
48. Psychological Testing & Counseling (free or low-cost assistance)
49. Race Relations (best sources for assistance)
50. Reading Remedial (free or low-cost assistance)
51. Recreation (primarily for out-of-town students)
52. Smoking withdrawal
53. Speech Therapy
54. Suicide Prevention
55. Transportation (know the what, how, and when of all forms of transportation for your school!)
56. Tutorial Services (free or low-cost assistance)
57. Venereal Diseases

You will add to this list if you really get involved with your students. And if you do, it will pay dividends in the form of thank-yous, retention, referrals, and lasting respect.

Chapter 21

Student Morale—
Creating It,
Keeping It!

According to Funk & Wagnall's Practical Standard Dictionary, MORALE is a state of mind with reference to courage, confidence, or hope, used especially of a number of persons associated in some enterprise such as troops, workers, or the like. From this definition we might conclude that morale is a good feeling—a sense of belonging, pride, and progress, a motivating feeling that nourishes the energies of a man or woman.

We have already covered much that is responsible for creating morale at any school. In this chapter we will touch on some of the many incidental items which contribute to the cumulative feeling that "We are #1."

Everyone likes to be on a winning team or to be associated with one. I am astounded at the bitterness of defeat so many people feel when their team loses. I similarly am fascinated by the exultation of those whose teams come out on top; you'd think each fan had personally knocked in the winning run or scored the go-a-head touchdown. I'm from Detroit. For years Detroiters had found it difficult to continue as ardent sports fans as we had to go back many years to recapture the magnificent joy of becoming the acknowledged best. Yet in 1968 Detroit was phenomenal, perhaps unique in all the history of a city's morale. It was a time of fear, of exodus and resentment. The smoke had scarcely cleared from the 1967 riot and the cinders of bigotry lay everywhere. Though temporarily subsided, emotions were as unsettled as an active volcano. No one was sure when the next eruption would occur, but almost everyone felt it most assuredly would.

Then a remarkable thing happened. The Detroit Tigers began to win baseball games. The daily topic of discussion was no longer just violence, but the anticipation of winning a pennant. More smiles appeared where somber mistrust had been for too long the mask of the Detroiter. Whether you knew first base from home plate didn't matter. You could not avoid the contagious enthusiasm of this marvelous disease. Tension drained swiftly with the approach of Fall. We got by the much-feared heat of summer, the catalyst of prior unrest and destruction. Minds were occupied with more important things, leading up to the American League pennant. It came to pass. So too did winning the World Series. People overwhelmed the streets on both occasions and the scene was reminiscent of a nursery school picnic. Color, race, religion, and social status were irrelevant. Everyone talked to everyone. A fan was a fan. How beautiful it was. And collectively we again began to admit we were from Detroit.

The emergence from the ashes of 1967 to the refurbished city of today had much to do with a state of mind. This in turn was largely inspired by twenty or so young men who liked to play games with a ball and a stick. And did it better than anyone else.

The morale you create at your school will certainly contribute to growth and satisfaction. And BEING THE BEST is the key.

We have already discussed the four motivating elements of human psychology. We may again use them to categorize the further suggestions you might use in your quest to excel.

RECOGNITION
Student pride of attendance is crucial. Conversely, if students are ashamed to admit they are attending your school you are in trouble. The following items are suggested as means of obtaining a distinct image of quality.

1. Every example of printed material should project an image of professionalism. Hire artists, professional sign men, copywriters, first class typesetters and knowledgeable printers. Don't convey a sloppy or second class image. Settle for nothing but first class.

   I've often seen schools go to the expense of creating an A-1 catalog, then send it out in an envelope that had the return address stamped angularly in the lefthand corner with the ink blurred. Mimeographed collateral material usually falls into the same demeaning category. Seldom legible, never indicative of a first class operation.

2. Figure out how to attract favorable newspaper editorials and time on local TV. When the opportunity arises make the most of it. Look and talk sharp. Plan what you are going to say and how you are going to say it!

3. Prepare a prestigious student identification card complete with color photo. Encase it in plastic.

4. Be selective in your recruitment. Make the student feel that he is indeed privileged to gain acceptance.

5. Consider the use of uniforms, shirts, hats, jackets, emblems, decals, which indicate the wearer is a member of a select group. Have a logo worthy of your aspirations.

6. Ask graduate students working in the field to address your classes, advising students on the significance and prestige of your diploma and how it opens doors to better employment opportunities.

   Norman Capps, Director of the Electronic Computer Programming Institute of Kansas City, makes a point of asking each visiting graduate to "step into the classroom for a minute." He reports very positive reactions.

7. Set up an Alumni Association and make sure your students are aware of the benefits of being accepted as members, through graduation.

8. Arrange for your students to get involved in community projects that may gain press and/or TV coverage. Examples might be manning telephones for fund raising marathons, charity walkathons, or bikeathons, judges in contests, assisting disadvantaged kids.

   When soliciting the media for these or other events, make sure you come up with an angle that is unique or unusual. Reporters from the media are seldom interested in "the same old thing." Create a story that is different and yet newsworthy and they'll beat a path to your door.

9. Line up local businessmen who will give a specific percentage discount to your students upon the presentation of the student identification card.

10. Initiate a "Graduate Hall of Fame" with ceremonies held annually, at which time the winners are announced. Plaques displayed in a designated area of your school can tell of the individual's accomplishments. Attending students will often aspire to do likewise.

ROMANCE

Make your school a more pleasant, exciting scene and place to be. Your effort will improve student morale. Don't forget that the happy student doesn't drop out if he can help it! And if he does, there's a good chance he'll be back. Consider these attractions:

1. A food-service operation. Whether with a restaurant, snack shop, or vending machines, when you feed stomachs you improve your chance to feed minds. Vary the menu often if possible.

2. Design more extracurricular activities—and produce a handsome schedule of these events so that students can anticipate future excitement. At the Wilma Boyd Career School of Pittsburgh, a social calendar is developed annually with the assistance of student counsel representatives. Among the traditional offerings are dances, swim parties,

and guided shopping trips. Common activities at schools throughout the country are picnics, sports tournaments, and bus trips to museums, sports events, tourist attractions, and scenic wonders. Needless to say, there are many other activities you might consider—but try to make them unique to your school, something very special.

3. Tie in recruitment with a social event. For example, a special party or weekend for these students who bring in two applicants who subsequently enroll (include their friends who enroll in the social event).

4. "Appreciation parties" are in general a way to say thanks and at the same time build morale. For instance, the Ohio Institute of Photography, Dayton, involved students in moving the school to a new location. Reports president Terry Guthrie: "We threw a Student Appreciation Party. We hired a band and supplied all the beer and snacks. During the party the staff filled the role of waiters and waitresses. Student problems inherent in such a move were forgotten."

5. School clubs created added interest and energy centers. President Jeanne Kretschmer of Detroit Business Institute, stresses the value of student involvement in clubs that encourage avocational interests. Hours assigned for club meetings become part of the school day (but not every day). The clubs are sponsored by the teachers, two to a club. On meeting days, those students who haven't joined a club are asked to go to the student hall.

6. Birthday cards, Christmas cards, get-well cards, sympathy cards mailed to students are a worthwhile investment, especially if the student's instructors sign them and add a personal note.

7. Newsletters prepared at regular intervals: mention as many students' names as possible in a favorable manner. Involve students in putting the paper together.

8. Have your continuing students attend the current graduation ceremonies; the pageantry may inspire some of them to persevere.

9. Friendly competition among classes. Announce the results in front of a school assembly. Recognition might be provided for best class attendance, best dressed class, class with cleanest home room, class with best decorated room (particularly appropriate for art schools), class most helpful to other classes, class taking the best care of tools and equipment. Let your ingenuity go to work; such recognitions can help to make every student feel more "at home" and motivated.

10. Don't be afraid to introduce even "corny" novelties into the school routine. For instance, a contest for "best dressed Irishman" on St. Patrick's Day (and everyone is Irish!), free cherry pies on Washington's Birthday to everyone who takes an oath to his or her honesty, free candy corn at Thanksgiving to everyone who will admit he or she is a Turkey, free whatever at Halloween for all who beg. Get the idea?

    Spread these crazy indulgences through the year. Not long ago, when the weather was dismal for a prolonged period, we noticed the long faces of many. We took small slips of paper and printed on them the following words: "Because you are smiling today you are entitled to a free coffee or coke at the restaurant. Present this slip." Our student counselor, chief instructor, office manager and a few others started handing them out at their discretion. Within minutes just about everyone was aware of being pleasant.

    Or again, as classes let out on the day before a vacation have your top administrators station themselves at the various exits. They simply shake hands with all the students as they leave, wishing them a nice holiday or whatever. It will take a few minutes, but it will really sell the perception that you sincerely care.

You can come up with innumerable ideas to build students' sense of participation. The important thing is to create events that are different and that bring students closer together, inspiring a student morale that is unique to your school. KEEP THINKING!

MONEY

It's no cinch for a student to concentrate on a lecture when his stomach is rumbling and he hasn't enough money to buy day-old pizza. Certainly it's a morale factor, and perhaps the most severe you will have to deal with. Do so promptly and confidentially. In addition, money—or the things money will buy—can be a positive morale factor in various ways:

1. Provide in-school jobs for those in immediate need. If maintenance work is not available consider brochure distribution. If your placement department or agencies can help, refer the student to a student counselor.

2. Offer prizes for perfect attendance. The names of all who haven't been late or absent are put into a hat. Winners are then drawn. Many schools offer prizes that are valuable in the careers being taught. Still others—such as Weslyn College of Medical and Dental Careers, Bellflower, California—believe a cash prize is the best recognition. A drawing is held each month. First prize is $15, second prize is $10 and third prize is $5. Don Jarrell, president says: "Granted, this is not a great deal of money, but it has created a lot of interest and fun for the students, and actually caused our attendance percentages to rise."

3. Some schools offer an actual cash award to those who continue to graduation. Where I am aware of this incentive it occurs in inner-city schools where dropout rates are usually much higher. From what I hear it has proven to be effective. However, I would strongly suggest contacting an attorney before initiating such a policy; there could be complications.

4. Distribute grant and loan funds that exceed tuition at frequent intervals. Although it is extra work, the weekly, bi-weekly, or monthly checks will help to keep students in school.

5. The financial aid people on your staff should be competent in all areas. Provide what is reasonable—but if possible, get the student to invest money in education. The student who is paying his or her own way will often possess a healthier outlook than the student who is totally subsidized.

SELF PRESERVATION

Students may be "turned on" by your training yet they will drop out if they must walk in fear. You have to provide the necessary assurances that no danger of physical harm exists, whether real or imagined. Consider the following items:

1. Outside security. Is your parking area fenced and is it well lighted? Is it a short or long distance from a car or public transportation to the doors of your school?

2. Security within your school. Is the entrance secured, or do non-students have easy access? Do you have crash-bars on your doors to prevent entry but allow exit? Do you allow students who have been found guilty of physical assertiveness to remain in school? Often a student may fear another student and leave without giving notice. Antagonism that will reach the level of violence or threats, however, usually can be spotted in advance. Alert your staff to the necessity for prompt action whenever arguments and hassle occur among students. If an open clash occurs a second time, both students involved should be referred to management for counseling.

3. Fire safety. Is each student aware of your fire alert system and the equipment you have to react quickly? Do you have fire extinguishers checked periodically? Do you have fire

drills? Particularly students who have had a bad experience with fire are sensitive to this area of safety.

4. Claustrophobia. This has more to do with student morale than you might think. Are you jamming too many into a classroom, so as to create a feeling of confinement?

5. Access to First Aid. Do you have first aid supplies on hand? Do your students know where they are? Are students aware of nearby professional medical assistance? Is the school equipped to assist students afflicted by chronic disorders?

6. Smoking. An increasing problem, as non-smokers stand up for their rights. Do you provide for their rights? If not, look into it. Seldom will this be the sole reason a student walks out, but it surely can contribute to it.

7. Chewing Tobacco. An alternative to smoking that can cause more classroom dissension than the chain smoker. The chewer unfortunately must spit and to many this is disgusting and non-sanitary. Best have a written regulation against it.

You, personally, may have no exaggerated fears or hang-ups about health or self-preservation. However, don't dismiss these concerns without due consideration. Psychiatrists don't drive Cadillacs as the result of inheriting their wealth.

Chapter 22

Should Students Interrupt—
Leave The Door Open

Early in my married life, my wife filled out one of those little "OK, tell me more" coupons circulated by a prominent encyclopedia publisher and it promptly brought a walking, talking version of the company's product to our door.

After a 30 minute soliloquy, in which he conveyed the idea that God would consult him before sending the next great floods, he asked for the order. In doing so he intimated that it was a shame to remain as ignorant as we were. And further, that we were surely not doing a favor to society by rearing our children in our own present image and likeness.

Having no weapons within reach, I conveyed an invitation to leave in what must have been the same tone of voice as Sam Huston used when talking to the contractor who forgot to put the rear exit in the Alamo.

Pausing at the door, he made one last statement: "If you allow me to walk through this door, you will never purchase encyclopedias!" I assured him I would allow him to leave. He slammed the door.

It really wasn't long afterward when we bought a set. As I recall, we signed the papers with a nice old lady who thought the books might be a joy to our obviously brilliant children!

Despite that first salesman's obvious ego problem, we might still have bought his very fine product had he not psychologically prevented us from doing so. The lesson here: "Don't make your goodbyes so final!"

When a student leaves your institution, let him do so with dignity. I don't want to infer we should not try to keep him in school, but if the writing is on the wall, don't let the final scene be one of hostility, accusation or bitterness.

Many parents have lost their children forever as a result of one angry outburst, "If you walk out that door now, don't ever bother to come back again!"

As school owners, we always hate to see anyone leave us, but as humanitarians, we also know that in some instances a temporary interruption is the most intelligent decision we can concur with. Maintaining the inflexible attitude that all interruptions are wrong is simply unrealistic. And should you belligerently cling to this philosophy through all your exit interviews, considerably fewer students will ever choose to return. Few of us care to revisit persons or places we associated with unpleasant emotional experiences. Fewer still go back to where we simply aren't wanted!

Should students interrupt—leave the door open!

Our goal should be to hold on to those we can hold on to—and to get the others to return as soon as they can, knowing they are welcome.

There is a major problem with this concept, and that is guaranteeing the opportunity to intelligently discuss the pros and cons with each student, before his or her decision is chiseled in stone.

Unfortunately, many students fear talking to school personnel about dropping out because they anticipate being hassled. It is so much easier to just not show up any more. "After all, they wouldn't understand the way I feel anyway!"

Students who lack the self-confidence to communicate their feelings will for the most part be similarly shy about returning, should they think about doing so at some future date. "They won't want me back, after the way I just walked out before!" Consider these means to encourage students to talk to you before departing:

1. As previously stated, advocate your concern every day in every way. Sell the student on the idea you're here to help, you're his friend, you're his hope. Develop the idea, through periodic counseling, that he or she can confide in you.

2. Provide written acknowledgement for classes completed. Whether a certificate or simply a letter, students can feel some pride in the training they did complete. Having this piece of paper is at least some proof to the world they are not complete failures.

3. Providing it doesn't violate either laws or accrediting standards, have a regulation that financially penalizes those who don't notify the school of their interruption.

So after all your efforts, the student has left. What next? It is surprising how little effort is made to get the student back in school once he has departed. Many schools will continue to invest sizeable amounts to get each new student, while they fail to invest 25¢ on the kid who dropped out, but who could return.

We suggest you establish a follow-up procedure for all those who have interrupted whom you would like to have return. Send out thought-provoking letters and notices at 30 day intervals.

Be sure to include in these contacts any dates before which they can return and avoid paying higher tuition rates. Keep this up for a year and it won't cost you much more than $3.

We don't need to consult Jimmy the Greek to determine the odds are in our favor—this investment will pay off! Particularly if we don't slam the door shut at the exit interview.

Chapter 23

Assisting The Slow Learner And Those In Need Of Remedial Assistance

Even though you may test for admission as well as require a high school diploma, there are few places in this country where you can be assured that competence in reading, writing, and arithmetic is at the appropriate level. Very truthfully, we have had applicants carrying high school diplomas who couldn't read or write one sentence of the English language. No, they didn't come to us with an I-20 form. They were the products of our public high schools.

Just saying "no" to these kids is hardly an answer, either for them, or us, or society. We therefore developed a working relationship with a private machine-oriented tutorial school. They test current levels of ability and give us the results at no charge. Applicants are then referred by us to schools which can assist them, and often to the school which tested them, with the promise they will be accepted by us when they raise their grade levels to a specific figure. The schools to which we refer students, in turn, keep us advised of all progress.

All this usually takes place prior to acceptance, but occasionally we find a student who is attending and does need help. The same procedure is followed with the exception of arranging hours of tutorial assistance that correspond with his occupational training.

Executive Director Hank Murray of Piedmont Aero Space Institute in Winston-Salem, North Carolina has worked out programs of remedial assistance with the county-operated Learning Center. He reports favorable results in science as well as in math and reading. But however you handle it, do research all of the sources of remedial education in your geographic area, and have this printed for handy reference and distribution.

Students with difficulty in reading comprehension can be encouraged to use a tape recorder. They can record their voice while reading any material, then listen to the replay. Or a friend or member of the family can read the text onto the tape. Either way, comprehension is made easier.

A few other principles you might try:

1. Establish your own remedial classes and charge tuition.

2. Build a library of cassette tapes which slow learners can take home.

3. Make your own video tapes of actual classroom lectures and demonstrations. Schedule monitored viewing at times other than class hours.

4. Arrange for slow learners to visit graduates working in the field, so they might get a better idea what is expected of them on the job. Of particular significance is having the graduate make the student aware of the necessity for continual reading and study so as to keep updated in his or her occupation.

5. Advocate specific living schedules so as to assure sufficient time for study. Hold classes on "Better Study Habits."

6. Recruit volunteers among your advanced students who would work with those having difficulty.

One final idea you might not have considered is new and fully valid course programs that avoid the math and reading skills a student needs to conquer present offerings. Courses, that is, in the same vein as you now offer, but easier; into which you can shift students as an alternative to termination.

Slow learners can be handled in much the same manner by gearing them to concentrate on a very specific but employable segment of a broad course offering.

As an owner of a proprietary school I always felt that if we accepted the student, then we accepted an obligation to train him or her for as long as the student's desire is obvious. If, after an extended period, we see mediocrity continue in all phases of the training, we will suggest to the student that he or she specialize. Thereafter, we will concentrate all our efforts to make the student employable in one phase of the profession. You might consider how this reasoning could apply to your offerings.

Chapter 24

The Inner-City Student

I was seated in my office on an ordinary day a year or so ago when I received a call from a secretary who advised me that her boss would be on the phone shortly to talk to me. Generally speaking, I think of bosses who flaunt their secretaries in such fashion as being very similar to guys who wear diamond rings on both hands. However, I waited.

"Mr. Diggs? This is Tom Jackson, head of the Mayor's Committee on Youth Development. We'd like you to bid on a training project for X number of inner-city kids, all of whom have dropped out of high school. You can probably earn some good money. The only requirement we stipulate is that you don't have over 5% drop out and that you guarantee jobs to all graduates!"

I can't remember when I have had as good a laugh.

Training dropouts to become participating members of society is a Mt. Everest challenge. One so difficult and complex that only the strong-hearted should attempt it. To teach a trade is not so much the problem; to get these people to the point where they can be taught is the awesome job! Schools that get into it solely for the money cannot possibly succeed.

When you accept inner-city students then you should also acknowledge the obligation to provide the necessary student services. This means more time, more patience, more effort, more creativity, and much more individualized attention. Before all else, each student must be encouraged to start believing in himself. Only then can occupational training begin to sink in.

The majority of students at the St. Louis Welding Institute are from the inner city. John C. Vatterott, the president, has picked up the gauntlet. And having lived with the frustrations inherent in such a student body, he has developed a mandatory "Survival Course." All students attend special sessions one hour each day for the first four weeks of training, and thereafter one hour each week for the duration of the course.

The extra sessions are organized in small groups. The net effect is to create conscious, mutually supportive clusters of students, who build their own spirit. While they do put each other through hoops, John reports that like brothers they also back up and encourage one another.

Mr. Vatterott's very helpful course outline is reprinted here in its entirety:

PROGRAM SURVIVAL

PHASE I

Week One:
- Tuesday: Get acquainted, discuss background of self and others.
- Wednesday: Lecture on first impression.
- Thursday: First impression and sense of pride
- Friday: Review of week and sense of pride.

Week Two:
- Tuesday: Discussion of group dynamics and group interaction.
- Wednesday: Role and meaning of work.
- Thursday: Competition, including positive and negative competition.
- Friday: Anger.

Week Three:
    Tuesday: Initial view of budgeting.
    Wednesday: Budgeting.
    Thursday: Frustration.
    Friday: Burnt toast.

Week Four:
    Tuesday: Discussion of graduation.
    Wednesday: Stress on a job.
    Thursday: Personal sense of pride.
    Friday: Review of Phase I.

PHASE II

Week Two: Discussion of uptight feelings on a scale of 1 to 10.

Week Three: Preparation for doing a job application and assertiveness training.

Week Four: Job application.

PHASE III

Week Two: Discussion of interviewing.

Week Three: Practice interviews.

Week Four: Plant politics.

PHASE IV

Week Two: Discussion of potential job sites.

Week Three: Review of first impressions and anger.

Week Four: Review interviewing, applications, and helpful hints.

PHASE V

Week Two:	Preparation for departure of 18 week students.
Week Three:	Discussion of feelings of separation.
Week Four:	Discussion of PHASE V.

PHASE VI

Week Two:	Review of job retention skills.
Week Three:	Review of interviewing techniques.
Week Four:	Review of plant politics and role and meaning of work.

PHASE VII

Week Two:	Final meeting: Discussion of pride and sense of accomplishment, deal with separation-anxiety blues.

For the school with relatively few students from the inner city, we suggest that if possible they be integrated into different classes so as to gain a social mix. These young men and women need both direction and inspiration, attitudes that may often be missing from a class comprised solely of those with similar backgrounds. I believe this is the reason why the Job Corps was such a failure. No one in the class could or would set the example.

Most of the ideas in this book are applicable to the inner-city student. There is little point in repeating, but we shall conclude with one reiterated thought. Until and unless you have a staff and, particularly, counselors who are willing to accept the heavier workload that accompanies the volume of attitudinal changes that you must make happen, stay away from recruiting the inner-city student! But God Bless those who do.

Chapter 25

Tuition—
Its Effect On
Attrition

Set it too high and students drop out! Set it too low and you can't provide the education or the necessary services—and students drop out! So what's the answer?

If I have my druthers, I'd rather be on the high side. Even the dropouts from a good school will take something with them they may ultimately use. The dropouts from a school that has curtailed education and services so as to "stay cheap" will carry with them only bad memories. These sour feelings may prevent them from ever returning to another school.

Maybe it is time for you to review your needs for additional staff, services, and equipment. If you could in fact better serve your students, establish the new budget accordingly. The important aspect of your tuition must be that the students get their money's worth—and that they feel this is so.

I personally can't visualize a graduate of any school saying, "Well, I didn't get much of an education but the price was right!"

Even if you ran a free school, supported by your own inheritance, but you failed to provide the education and services necessary to turn out a student capable of remunerative employment, you'd be bad-mouthed by every kid who walked out of your door.

Throughout this country, hundreds of community colleges offer similarly titled courses to those provided at proprietary schools. Often they're almost next door. And yet the proprietary schools prosper although the community college is much less expensive. How can this be? Ultimately, quality and concern tell the story.

To shop for an education is like the search for a doctor to perform surgery. The consumer is rightly concerned about your past successes. I can't visualize anyone choosing a non-experienced heart surgeon—with an attitude of, "Well, maybe everything will be okay"—in order to save a few dollars.

Be a specialist with an enviable reputation. Set your tuition so this can become possible.

Will you engender some dropouts? Probably a few. But when they've saved enough to return to school, it could well be your school they'll prefer to re-enter!

Chapter 26

Support Vocational Education —And The Job Done By Proprietary Schools

My memories of Mrs. Roy are still vivid. She was my totally dedicated 8th grade homeroom teacher. A wonderful, giving woman of sixty or so, her every initiative was directed toward the success of her students. She laid down the law in no uncertain terms. But her motives were unmistakeable. Her concern for each of us was obvious. And we all loved her.

As was—and is—the fault of many teachers, however, she tried to reshape each student into her own image.

I can hear her now. "Better hit those books, young man. What do you want to settle for becoming? A mechanic?" She meant no harm.

Nor have the thousands of other educators who in one way or another have insinuated that the trades are undignified. Yet the harm was done. Hollywood picked up those stereotypes, and really did a job in convincing the nation that nobody with half a brain wore anything but a white shirt. And trade schools were for dummies. Everybody knew that. But then, what else could one do with the Gomer Pyles of the earth?

Well, as you know the pendulum has swung back. The wages paid to those who work with muscles and with hands have escalated. So too the salaries paid for numerous jobs traditionally set apart as women's work. With the raises has come more respect. Much remains to be done, however, as long as there continues to be cancellations because "Dad or Mom doesn't want me to go into this field."

Stand up for every segment of Occupational Education, and get your state associations working to promote salaries and stature!

While we are on the subject of standing up for a deserving cause, perhaps it's time this country began to salute the astounding contribution made to the nation's welfare by private occupational schools over the last century and more. Few segments of free enterprise have as dramatically impacted the industrialization of this country. And today these private schools are no less a force. No individual in this country spends one day of his life without somehow being served or affected by those who acquired their skills in a private occupational school.

Private schools first supplied the need for formal occupational training in the nineteenth century. Private schools have sustained the airline industry from its infancy to its present attainments. Private schools trained the first typists and clerical personnel. Private schools trained the early radio repairmen, then the TV industry's repairmen. Private schools quickly began to qualify personnel for the infant computer industry. Over the years the vast majority of auto mechanics have learned their trade in private schools. So, too, have truck drivers, heavy-equipment repairmen, and those in refrigeration, welding, and meat cutting.

Did you ever stop to think that without the proprietary occupational schools, our hospitals would be devoid of trained personnel, the fashion industry might have us still wearing knickers and babushkas, and some relative would be trying to cut our hair with the use of a cereal bowl? Without proprietary instruction, few trained personnel might be available to draft or wire or fix our machinery, create our floral displays, or perform hundreds of other services.

This training has been conceived and rendered available by individuals with vision, people with dreams who made them come true in the framework of the system of free enterprise. Unfortunately, there are many who have lost sight of how this country gained greatness. They speak about profits in much the same way they would of a flu epidemic from Hong Kong—dangerous to our National Health! About profit in education their vehemence is even greater.

I have often thought how emphatic and decisive a story we could tell, if every worker in this country who learned his or her skills in a proprietary school just stayed home from work one day! This country would virtually come to a screeching halt.

That's unrealistic. Sure it is; but there are other ways that the story can be communicated.

Not long ago, a Detroit TV Station ran a weeklong series of broadcasts on proprietary schools. Most of the material presented was right out of Washington and far from complimentary. Monday and Tuesday passed without so much as a kind word, before representatives from the Michigan Organization of Private Vocational Schools contacted the station with one simple request: "Please survey your own personnel to find out how many of your employees learned their skills in a private occupational school." They agreed. The results came too late to alter Wednesday's show, but Thursday and Friday turned the entire week into quite another story. They found that over 70% of all their technical people were the products of private schools, as well as many of the clerical staff and some of the talent.

Across the country, most proprietary schools are small. Being small, however, allows them to be more personal with each student and consequently more successful. But as small schools are more productive, they are also more vulnerable. Few schools, if any, have the size and backing to lobby successfully at the state level, let along Washington.

If you aren't actively involved with your state and national associations, become so. Collectively, these schools can tell a dramatic story. A Story that could do much to silence those who periodically question the integrity of this industry on the basis of hearsay isolated incidents taken out of context, or unclarified assumptions.

Your efforts on behalf of the Private School Industry as a whole, could well prevent some cancellations and dropouts.

It is sad to realize that students will cancel or drop out because of the embarrassment and ridicule they may be subjected to because they enrolled at a private occupational school; but it has happened! And it will continue to happen, as long as this industry remains silent.

Work hard for yourself, and your students, and your industry. You'll help to preserve the free-enterprise society. This country can ill afford a state-run monopoly of eductation. The price that would exact, the risk that would run, is fearful to contemplate!

Chapter 27

When Dropping A Student Is Advisable

I once read this very profound statement: "A recent study has proven that 50% of all statistics are useless."

Although I estimate that the percentage of worthless data is actually considerably higher, this hasn't dampened the government's enthusiasm to request information with ever increasing frequency. As a result, no school director can operate without a very high awareness of certain facts and figures. The attrition rate certainly constitutes one of these tender areas.

As a consequence of a student's premature departure, resentment may surge up in the breast of the school official. Mostly it is salutary he or she feels this way. Quite as often, however, our desire for favorable statistics blinds us to the possible advantages of recording an occasional dropout.

For despite our attempts to limit the access to our schools to those who possess the aptitude, intelligence, and motivation, we all accept a certain number who, in our opinion, should be residing at the local funny farm.

To hang onto these people after repeated attempts to shape, direct, communicate, and motivate have failed is downright foolish. It is particularly stupid if the problem-child's behavior is causing dissension, fear, chaos, or morale problems within the classroom.

Why go looking for the lost sheep if it means loss of the flock? There comes a time when saying goodbye may be the wisest thing to do. Delay can result in multiple student losses as well as injury to our institutional reputation.

To interrupt a student for unsatisfactory progress can be similarly agonizing, but it must be done. The alternative is to undercut school philosophy. This hypocrisy is evident to any student body. The students will judge you "capable of doing anything to make a buck." It is counterproductive, and can lead to more attrition than you ever anticipated in addition to eroding the community respect necessary to maintain your image.

And the reverse is true. To wish Godspeed to a student who voluntarily decides to pursue an alternative to your courses is no easy decision. But it can work eventually to your advantage.

Some years ago, we accepted a black ex-convict. He had spent almost half his thirty-some years behind bars. There were few crimes short of murder he hadn't committed, and it didn't take too long to realize he was far from having been rehabilitated. His bitterness towards authority and particularly white authority was obvious. He never smiled. His eyes narrowed and his jaw rigidly locked in place at the least apprehension. It was sad. We thought: "How could we possibly place this man even if we manage to train him?"

Soon the first trouble arose. Another black student came into my office and said, "I think you ought to know that Nate is planning to take your secretary's car after class and see the town and he ain't got a driver's license." I thanked him, then checked with my secretary. She said she was trying to sell the car and had posted a notice to that effect on the bulletin board. Nate had inquired about buying it and said he would be back after class to take a test drive.

I called Nate into my office and asked him if what I had heard was true,—that he did not have a driver's license! His eyes narrowed, as he let loose a fusilade of four letter words combined with some lengthier inferences about my heritage. He ended his tirade with the unmistakable opinion that it was none of my business.

Although not the model of internal composure, I did manage to calmly inquire why he didn't avoid the possibility of further problems with the law—by getting a license. His demeanor changed little as he continued to color the air blue with his choice of words. He did explain, however. He presently had six warrants out for his arrest and by no means was he going near a police station!

I offered to help as I knew a few judges. I strengthened my offer by asking if he intended to run all his life? He quieted down considerably—then in so many words offered a defiant challenge. You want to help? Prove it

After obtaining a pretty good list of Nate's problems I called Judge Maher. I explained that I felt we could save Nate. The judge agreed to do what he could. Nate was to appear before him that Thursday. Nate agreed to go!

Early the following Saturday, the phone rang. I arose to answer it. A female and obviously black voice asked: "Is this the Mr. Diggs that runs the school?" I said yes. She said, "I've got a message for you from Nate." I said, "Yes." She said, "When he gets out he's gonna kill you!"

You know, there's something about a statement like that which prompts every function in the human body to simultaneously awaken.

Come to find out, the docket was too full on Thursday. Nate was asked to return on Friday. The judge, in a mental lapse, promptly sentenced him.

I awoke the judge. "My God, did I do that?" he said. "I must be getting old, I forgot all about him!" The judge gave me his word he would get him out first thing Monday morning. There wasn't much he could do until then.

His word was good. Nate came walking in shortly before noon. Two of the warrants had been cleared up. He didn't exactly appear friendly, but he sure wasn't violent. He just stared. I said, "Okay, what's next?"

As I recall it was about five months later when we walked out of the final courthouse after clearing up every last warrant against him. He turned to me and said, "I still can't believe a white man would help me out!—Thanks."

From that day on, Nate was a super student. Besides that, he smiled and began to communicate. I sure was proud, but not as proud as the day he came to me and said he was going to drop out. To take a job with the state, counseling inner-city kids.

Sure he would have made a fine mechanic. But in terms of his value to society, there was little doubt that the counseling job was the right decision. And something he really wanted to do. I encouraged him.

The joy of helping this student dropout didn't really surface until a year or so later. I hadn't heard from Nate in at least a dozen months when one day he called. "Mr. Diggs, this is Nate. I need your help. Our agency is out of funds but I've got a guy who could really benefit from your training. Is there any chance of getting him a scholarship?" I said, "Sure, Nate, send him out." He came. He was white.

There have been many other times when I've had to agree with a student's decision to leave because of opportunities he or she was prone to accept prior to completion of a course. I had only to ask myself, what would I do."

I sure didn't like the idea of having another statistic that, to some, indicated a failure. But at the same time I was comforted in knowing that, my pleasure and purpose as an educator wasn't merely to gratify those who analyzed numbers on annual reports.

To summarize, about the only way dropouts like this will hurt you is statistically. Money-wise you'll only benefit. Ridding yourself of the chronic trouble-maker will save others in the class. Encouraging those who sincerely do have unusual opportunities can only result in being the recipient of many confident referrals.

Conclusion

The fact that you have read this far indicates you already possess the right attitude to improve your retention rates. What is necessary now is a plan,—a comprehensive plan. It should be spelled out in detail, typed, and then circulated for all staff members to digest.

Convincing all your staff to abruptly adopt an altruistic approach in their careers will be no simple task. But if you carefully explain that their future wages may well depend on the success of your plan, it will certainly help.

To prepare your plan, try re-reading each chapter with a pencil in your hand and a good-sized legal pad in front of you. Have your employees do the same, each writing down ideas as they occur, and expressing opinions about the possible effectiveness of the guidelines and suggestions offered by this book.

You, as an administrator, will find it consistently easier to advocate new policy, if the content of that policy is determined by staff suggestions.

Advise the staff of the results gained in each phase of implementing a retention plan. Progress is always worth sharing; and everyone likes to know that his or her efforts have been valuable.

Follow this advice, and your statistics will take care of themselves. Particularly that statistic which should mean more to you than any other: "Our staff gives 100%."

RICHARD N. DIGGS

ABOUT THE AUTHOR

Richard Diggs is widely recognized for his contributions to the proprietary vocational sector of American education. A product of Detroit's parochial system and the University of Detroit, he has worked in numerous diverse positions which have included being a stock broker, bank department manager, night club comedian, College Director, magazine editor, and freelance writer.

In addition Mr. Diggs has owned ten very distinct corporations including several proprietary occupational schools, an advertising agency, two retail operations, a manufacturing company, a business consulting firm, and a publishing company.

Since 1965 Mr. Diggs has devoted almost all his time to some aspect of post-secondary education. He was twice elected President of The Michigan Association of Private Schools, served on The Advisory Council on Adult & Continuing Education for the State of Michigan, and served for years on The Governor's Commission of Higher Education.

Mr. Diggs served as a member of the accrediting commission for The National Association of Trade & Technical Schools from 1972 through 1978, was Education Officer for the Region 5 Executive Committee of HEW under Dr. Mousolite, and founded The Michigan Organization of Private Vocational Schools.

Married with three children, Mr. Diggs is an acclaimed public speaker and author. In addition to *Keeping Students from Dropping Out*, first published in 1978, he wrote *Michigan's Private Occupational Schools* (1975), and seven books on the science of getting a job. These have included *Getting the Job You Want at the Wage You Know You Deserve* (1968), *The Great Job Hunt* (1985), *Employability . . . Plus* (1987), and *Finding Your Ideal Job* (1988).

Keeping Students From Dropping Out. $17.95

ARE AMERICA'S SCHOOLS
failing their students?

CAN AN EDUCATOR, A TEACHER, AN
ADMINISTRATOR DO ANYTHING
single-handedly to reverse the attrition trend?

CAN A SYSTEM be made of good ideas for
preventing dropouts?

CAN AN EXPERIENCED EDUCATOR still
pick up, or remember, good ideas?

HAS THE PRIVATE SECTOR OF JOB
EDUCATION anything — or a lot — to impart
to the public educational sector?

WHAT IS THE EQUATION between
preventing dropouts and increasing enrollment
levels?

*This book provides unique answers to these
questions, supplied by a uniquely practical
figure in American education.*